Seven Days to Say
I Love You

Copyright Ashley Hames 2011

This is a work of non-fiction based on the life, experiences and recollections of the author.

The contents of this book are true.

For Elisa

In memory of my father

DAY ONE

Coming Home

Today my Dad is coming home from hospital; he has just been diagnosed with terminal cancer.

My Mum drove off earlier in the morning to gather him up and bring him back home to the place he loves and where he will now spend his final days.

I sit and wait; I wonder how I should greet him when he arrives. I want to make him feel better, to help him, and to let him know that all I want is for him to be OK. I dread and yet long for him to walk through the doors of the house and for me to let him know that I am here for him. I think about what might happen when my parents return: *'Welcome home, Dad,'* is all I really want to say as I hug him and hold him for a few brief seconds before helping him upstairs to bed.

I hear a car park up outside and I reckon it's probably my parents. I get up and walk through the hallway where my suitcase still lies unopened from my return the previous night. I open the door. The cold air hits me and with it the neat scenario that I'd mapped out is gone in an instant. Dad is walking slowly, precariously down the pavement with Mum holding his arm as support. He looks weak, haunted and hurt. I worry for a fraction of a second that he may be seen by the other people living on the street – I don't want them to see my father like this – I want this to be a private moment where he is given peace; I want him to be left alone as he reaches the final days of his sixty seven year old life.

He is wearing pyjamas and my blue dressing gown which Mum had borrowed from me earlier that day. His shoes are dragging on the pavement a little. He's walking, shuffling, and you can tell he's struggling to keep moving, to stay upright. I'm scared he may fall over. Christ, please let him be alright.

In the clear daylight he looks extremely ill – worse than he had appeared to be when I had visited him in hospital the day before. He has terminal liver cancer and his skin has turned yellow with jaundice. Even the whites of his eyes are stained with yellow. But they are piercing and bright in the sunlight.

This all seems so awful. But this is really happening and it's a real nightmare being played out in the small country village of Much Wenlock, in the heart of Shropshire, England.

Dad sees me as I lean out from the door.
'Hello Dad.'
He struggles to lift an arm to greet me.
'Hey Ash.'
He's focusing strongly on trying to stay on his feet. That's what's important to him now. He doesn't want to fall over. He doesn't want me getting in the way. Although he's walking slowly I can see that he's rushing. He wants to get in the house and get to bed. Get this over with.

He and Mum go past me and through the front door. Now they have to go upstairs. I stay silent and, wanting to help and afraid that my father may stutter and fall, I follow them up the stairs, a couple of paces behind. It's anguish. I feel like I'm holding my breath.

They make it to the top of the stairs and for a second or two, my Dad stops and leans on the top of the banister. A few more paces and he will be in the bedroom. Mum opens the door and Dad slowly rushes, staggers towards her. As he nears the finishing line he's completely exhausted and he collapses head first onto the surface of the bed.

God, I feel so sorry for him. I hate his helplessness. I just want everything to be better. Mum is reassuring him and moves to take his shoes off and get him comfortable. Dad stays still for a while. His legs are half-dangling off the end of the bed. He's a spent force and needs to rest, to catch his breath. After a minute or two his breathing slows down he is ready to ease his way up the bed and Mum later settles him beneath the duvet.

Dad is now home, and we will now prepare for his death.

The Diagnosis

I had spoken on the phone to my sister, Rebecca, a couple of weeks before when I heard for the first time that Dad was not feeling well. Rebecca had gone home for the weekend and a couple of days after she left, Dad had been taken to hospital where he had undergone a routine operation to remove a gall stone. He returned home believing the problem had been dealt with, but a few days later he deteriorated further and was taken back to hospital.

I called Mum to see how things were and she told me that Dad was having some more tests done over the next few days to try and find out what was wrong with him. She sounded worried and suggested that I call my father on his mobile and have a chat.

When my Dad picked up the phone from his hospital bed, the voice on the other end of the line was faint and hoarse. I was quite shocked: He did not sound well. The more I spoke to him, the more I grew concerned. Not only did he sound extremely weak, but rather than having a normal, carefree conversation, Dad was trying to give me worldly words of wisdom concerning my career. This was nothing particularly out of character – his tendency to preach to me and my siblings had previously earned him the nickname 'The Vicar'. Usually his sermons were amusing and would have prompted some light mockery; but this time, combined with his being in hospital and the frailty of his voice, it jarred.

I went to bed that night and woke in the early hours with worry. What if my father was seriously ill? I had had no major crisis in my life to deal with – and I didn't feel prepared for something going wrong at the heart of our family. We had lived a fairly charmed middle-class English life. My parents had been married for over forty years. We all got on, we were healthy. My brother and sister and I were friends. But how would we handle things if Dad was to disappear from our lives?

The next day, I spoke to Mum on the phone from my flat in London – they would get Dad's test results on Thursday. Again, I felt something of real concern in Mum's voice; something didn't feel right.

Another restless night follows; I wake in the early hours and start thinking things through. I feel like I somehow need to brace myself for something bad; get my head in the right place, to mentally prepare for the worst. But why am I thinking like this? There's nothing to really indicate that anything genuinely serious was affecting my father, but a sixth sense, instinct - perhaps hearing him so weak on the phone - is telling me that he is not well, that we could be heading for disaster, that tragedy was on its way.

What if my father died? How would we cope with that? But he couldn't die could he? He would be fine; he'd only been feeling ill for a week and I was fretting about something that hadn't happened yet and probably wouldn't happen for years to come. He'd never really been ill before – he'd lived a fit and healthy life. But the thought that things might not turn out all right stayed with me. I returned to sleep and woke up the next morning having already decided to go home the following day.

I called Mum to let her know my plans so she could pick me up from the train station. Again, her voice sounded heavy with concern.

'Well, it'll have to be sometime in the afternoon because your father will be getting his test results in the morning.'

I would be travelling back home to Shropshire from London, where I had been living for the past fifteen years.

I pack up and leave my flat, put my headphones on and listen to music for the few hours it takes to travel up North. My mind is blank and the time passes quickly. Then I am at Telford train station and I walk over the platform bridge and head down to the car park where I see my Mum's car.

She opens the door, gets out and I can sense immediately that it's very bad news. Her eyes tell a million words as she walks quietly over to me. I put my bag down and she's standing opposite me. My stomach tightens.

'I'm afraid your father is extremely ill.'

Those are the words that have just turned our lives upside down. We hug. I want to stay strong for my mother.

'It's OK Mum, I know. It's alright.'

I hold her for a second. Mum has tears in her eyes. I think she's been crying. She seems so small and fragile and her heart is being ripped apart.

Dad has been diagnosed with terminal liver cancer. The doctors have told him he has a matter of weeks rather than months to live - my Dad is about to die and there's absolutely nothing any of us can do about it.

    Mum and I will go and visit him later that afternoon.

In Hospital

I walk into hospital and over in the far corner of the ward I can see my Dad. I go over to him. He's lying in bed on his side and hasn't seen me yet.

'Hi Dad,' I say.

He doesn't look all that terrible for someone with a death sentence hovering over him, but he is quite obviously very ill. His skin is jaundiced; his movements are slow and strained. He shifts around to greet me.

'Hey Ash.'

'Good to see you Dad.'

I ask him about what the doctors have told him and he lifts down the sheet on top of him to show me his arms and chest which are virtually fluorescent in colour. It's alarming to see but I'm glad he feels free to show me.

I ask him how he's feeling and he says,

'OK really.'

'That's good,' I say.

But I really want to know about how he's feeling inside though, about the fact that he's not got much time left. I don't want this left unsaid, it needs to be dealt with and I somehow want to try and set the tone where we talk things through openly, so I go ahead and ask him outright.

'But how are you feeling about what you've been told Dad?'

He immediately reassures me.

'I have no problem with it. Honestly, I'm perfectly OK with it.'

In spite of the bombshell he has just received, Dad, as usual, is being really positive and brave. He is totally lucid, has accepted his fate and wants us to believe that it's alright that he has so little time left.

'Really, I'm absolutely fine with it, Ashley. You always said to me that you never wanted to last beyond seventy. Well, I'm only a few years off that.'

I wonder later if he really meant this – that he was content with what he'd been told. Surely, inside, he was screaming with frustration and fear but perhaps wanted to say the things we wanted to hear, to help make us more accepting of his fate. Maybe this was his consolation: that by saying he was alright and making us believe him, then he could find contentment with that.

But it's also true what my father says – I had always been very wary of growing old and the thought of staggering into old age had always frightened me – seventy, as my Dad had mentioned, was my cut-off point.

Now though, with the reality of my own father's condition in front of me, that seems far too young to die. Dad, I think, has so much more to give.

He smiles at me and I can tell that he is really happy to see me. He asks me my news and I tell him a few details but it all seems so utterly insignificant. I have no other desire other than to make sure he is OK and that he is feeling calm and relaxed. Nothing else matters now.

Still, I give him news about a book I have written and tell him that it's going to be published in a few months' time.

'Good luck with that,' he says.

And that one sentence kills me because I know he's saying that because he won't be around to see it. Dad had always wanted me to write and now that I finally have a book about to hit the shelves he will never get to hold it, see it or read it. I selfishly hate the fact that he will not be alive for the release date. It won't be out for another three or four months and that will be too late for him. I hate death for that. It's the first time I will resent death for making things so much worse for me. But for the moment, what matters is not how this will affect me - what matters is Dad and how he's feeling; what matters is how my Mum is taking this and how she is going to be when it's all over.

Mum is busy nursing my father; she takes a flannel and douses it in cold water and places it on my father's forehead. He has hot sweats and needs to be cooled down. His body is hurting, it's closing down, and he's taking oral doses of morphine to ease the pain and discomfort. Cancer is growing inside him. It may have already been there for several months and now it's too late for him to be treated.

Liver cancer, Mum later tells me, is known as the silent killer. There are no real symptoms until it's too late. And this silent killer is now its going to kill my Dad. He will be another victim, another cancer statistic, a real live breathing human being eaten alive by a disease with no real cure.

But I don't want to know about the cancer or any other medical details – what's done is done and all I care about is that my Dad is feeling alright, that he's comfortable, that he is not in too much pain. I want to ignore the cancer, to treat this intruder with contempt. If I show any curiosity about the disease I will be getting to know it, and I don't want to know it. I don't want to dignify it with acknowledgement. All I know is that it is going to be my father's cause of death and that's the only detail that matters. The rest of it is just noise and confusion.

Considering that only hours ago he's been told that he will die in a matter of weeks, my father is in good spirits, or at least he is making an enormous effort to appear at ease. I feel ridiculously proud of him. He is being how he has always been – pragmatic, thoughtful, sweet, dignified.

Mum and I end our visit and leave Dad to spend another night in hospital. We hate leaving him there, but my Mum has spoken about getting him home within the next couple of days. The doctors want to stabilise him and get him on the right dosage of drugs to balance out the pain and keep him well enough to still be able to eat. At the moment he is being sick a lot, unable to keep his food down because the combination of drugs isn't quite right yet.

We go out to the dreary grey car-park of Shrewsbury hospital. We get in the car and I ask Mum how she is feeling.

'I just can't believe this is actually happening. It doesn't seem real at all.'

And that's exactly how I feel. It's such a huge slice of information to take in that somehow my brain seems unable to connect with the magnitude, the enormity of what we are now facing. Everything seems so surreal and I'm not quite sure what to think. How is it normal to react in these circumstances?

As we set off I can see that although Mum is driving, her mind is back at Dad's bedside and she is very distracted. I mention this to her so she doesn't have an accident - the last thing we need is to prang the car and have a mini-crisis to deal with rather than with what's important. I'm trying to think practically, trying to focus...trying to think a bit like Dad.

We make it safely back home and get on with normal things like unpacking, cooking, eating. I switch on the television and laugh out loud at something I'm later watching. *How can I still be able to laugh?*

The First Goodbye

The following day we head back to see Dad. One of my younger cousins, Nina, has also arranged to visit him after we get there. Mum and I arrive at the hospital; we wipe our hands with the disinfectant provided outside the ward where Dad is staying and then walk in to see him. He is lying down in bed facing the window.

'Hello Hamesy,' says Mum as we walk over to his bed.

Dad stirs and I greet him as well.

'Hi Dad; you alright?'

He quite plainly is not alright but these are still the questions that you find yourself asking without it somehow feeling completely stupid.

He strains to lift his head up a little and smiles as we come into view.

'Hey Ash, how are you?'

'Good; how are you feeling today?'

Dad tells us he has not been sleeping very well and is still unable to eat much without throwing it up immediately afterwards. His mouth is also very dehydrated and he keeps licking his lips as he's speaking to try and lubricate them. I pass him a juice from the end of his bed and he sips a little to ease the difficulty of talking with such a dry mouth.

Mum helps him to sit up in bed and puts a pillow behind him to prop him up: she has gone into nurse-mode. The view from the window is of grey rooftops and the hospital car-park. It makes me want to get him home as soon as possible. Hamesy, as my Dad is known, was keen to get back that same day but after talking to Mum they both decide it's better to try and get him discharged tomorrow because he is being sick so much. The Doctors want to keep an eye on him and Mum is keen to get the medication more balanced so he can start eating a bit more and not just throw it straight back up.

It's coming up to three o' clock when my cousin Nina is due to arrive so I tell Dad I'm going to go outside to meet up with her and bring her up to see him. I get up to leave slightly earlier than I have to because I really want to leave Mum and Dad alone together. I want them to have as much time as possible on their own because time, time is running out. Looking at Dad and sensing how he's feeling, I just know he is not going to be alive for that much longer.

I go to the lift and wait outside for Nina. Before long, she arrives and we hug and go back into the hospital together. I take her over to Dad and she settles at his bedside and talk. I know this is going to be the last time they will ever speak together.

Nina tells him she is due to leave in a couple of days for a holiday in Las Vegas with her husband Russell. Dad wishes her a safe trip and asks her where she is staying. I can't help wondering why they're not talking about deeper stuff – like life and death and cancer and God and things that really matter. I feel myself wanting to step in and urge that they cut out the small talk - but I'm being stupid and naïve - this isn't Hollywood, this isn't clichéd: it's real life and it's not easy or neat and tidy or necessarily significant or meaningful. Besides, I don't even know what matters anymore anyway – all I know is that Dad is ill and that is making me upset.

I head off to the toilet because I don't want Dad to see me crying. I need to compose myself.

As I walk back, it's nearly time for Nina to leave. She leans over to kiss my father and says goodbye. Both of them begin to cry and it's the first time I have seen Dad in tears since his mother's funeral some ten years ago. He seems so powerless. We're all powerless.

Nina stands up, walks over to my Mum and they embrace. Mum, who has been holding herself together can do so no longer and I see her face crease into tears. She looks so small, so vulnerable and I can't bear to see what's happening in front of me. Nina turns towards me and I put my arm around her shoulder and lead her away.

This has been the first of Dad's last goodbyes. I can't even begin to imagine how he's feeling. I drop Nina off and as I head back to his bedside, I'm dreading the thought of seeing him upset and in tears. I turn the corner to enter his ward and he looks over to me, smiles and throws me a wink. I absolutely love him for that and I fill up with pride.

To me, that wink says *'Son, I'm in a bad place, but I'm cool with it.'*

That wink helps to sum up my Dad for what he was: a really kind, sweet and loving guy with a great sense of humour and a laid back, classy attitude to life. He was bright and switched on but above all, totally selfless.

Mum and I stay a while longer and then we must go. Mum will come back again tomorrow to see

Dad in hospital for the last time and bring him home. We walk out together and I say to Mum how amazed I am at how well Dad appears to be dealing with his situation. It seems he has come to terms with the hand he's been dealt.

'It's not really him who has the problem with his illness,' I say. 'It's us.'

Mum agrees by saying that it doesn't surprise her in the slightest, that this is how Dad has always been – practical, philosophical, thinking positive.

Tomorrow then, Dad will be coming home. He has quite rightly decided that he wants to be at home for the final weeks of life and then, when the right moment comes, to be transferred to the local hospice where he will die.

I am so glad he is coming home and will not be staying in hospital. I want him out of there desperately. I want him back where he belongs, back at home with his family. I don't want him surrounded by illness or nurses or trolleys or wheelchairs. I want him to be in the clear air of home, away from the smell of disinfectant. I want him to be able to see out of the window and to hear the birds sing.

I want him back home with me and Mum.

Looking Back

It's now over six months since Dad has died, and I still feel a ridiculously strong, intense sense of loss. For now, and I suspect forever, it seems like there's no such thing as a full recovery.

I feel vulnerable at any moment.

Back in London, I find myself on the tube sitting opposite a father and his two young daughters. The children are laughing as their Dad nuzzles them and bounces them on his knee. One of the children is looking at me and I feel like breaking down and having a bit of a cry. One day her father will die and she doesn't know that yet.

I hate that tragedy lies in wait for everyone.

When I am back with Mum in the weeks after Dad has died, I will be sitting in the lounge and suddenly I hear something and become convinced I have just heard my father's voice. I know it sounds crazy but I run over to the other side of the room to look out of the window and see if he's there. But no, just a few passers-by are walking down the street outside. It was nothing.

Another time after his death, I will be coming back from the shops and a car is approaching me and I can see my father sat in the driver's seat. I stop and stare and the car slows down to turn into the road at the junction where I am standing and I can then see clearly that it is someone else.

I will never see my father again, nor will I ever hear his voice.

Back in my flat in London, I wake one morning from a nightmare: in it, Mum and I have been chatting in the kitchen of the cottage where we used to live for the first thirty years of my life. Mum then turns to me and completely out of the blue says,

'Ashley, I'm afraid your father died last night.'

She comes over to me and hugs me .The news hits me like a juggernaut: I shout out 'No!' and break from my mother's embrace. I am hyperventilating and so I bend over double in an effort to gather in oxygen. I feel myself suffocating. And then I wake up, open my eyes and find I am crouched into a ball and am breathing very heavily in my bed. I will relax for a second and thank God that this is just a nightmare and then with bottomless disappointment I will realise that although I have been dreaming, the bigger truth is still the same.

I know I've been lucky, that I was blessed with a father that I could love and who was kind, generous, supportive and encouraging and all the great attributes that good fathers can have. But then it has to end and you're left with a space that can't be filled.

I almost resent my run of good fortune – if life hadn't been so kind to me and Dad hadn't been such a decent guy then maybe his death would possibly have been easier to accept. But it's been months now since my Dad died and I still can't really get to grips with it. It's just too enormous a burden; it's something that I can't put my arms around to feel or understand.

But if I think I'm fighting a tough battle, then how must things be for my Mum? I'm continually worried about her. When I cry, I don't just cry for my Dad any more, I cry for my Mum. I don't want her to be alone. I can't stand the thought of her returning home to an empty house. To think of her sitting down to eat an evening meal on her own breaks my heart.

Now, with my Dad's death, she has been sentenced to - who knows how much? - time bereft of the companionship she probably took for granted just a very short time ago. What's going through her mind as she settles down to bed for another lonely night? She and Dad were married for over forty years; they spent very little time apart. What's that like when the person you have chosen to spend your life with suddenly disappears from view? How do you recover? Do you ever recover or do you just...*adapt*?

DAY TWO

English Reserve

Dad has been home for a day now and Mum and I seem to have adjusted quickly into caring for Hamesy, as we call him. He seems no better or worse since he got back, but it's great that he's now with us at home. I love knowing that he is upstairs and that he can hear Mum and I getting on with life. When I ask him if he wants me to close the bedroom door, he insists he likes it kept open. He wants to hear us. He wants the sounds and smells to come up and cast a warm glow around him. He wants to feel a part of things, and he is.

My bedroom is upstairs from my parents' room. In the early hours of my first night home I wake up with a jolt and - for a fraction of a second - relief pours through me that, like in a film, the last couple of days had all been a bad dream. But dread and helplessness immediately take hold of me as reality hits, and I suddenly realise that the nightmare is true: this really is happening – my Dad is in the process of dying downstairs and there's nothing I can do to change anything.

I have been awake for three or four seconds and I am already crying.

During the following days, I will wake in the mornings and almost as quickly as my eyelids open, I have a leg out of the bed as I make a move to get up. My first and only thought is whether Dad is OK, and that I have to go and see him and make sure he's alright. I can't bear the thought of him being distressed.

Mum is the same: we are both on auto-pilot; all hands on deck.

I get dressed and walk downstairs, stopping to take a look at Dad. He is sleeping alone because Mum has now had to move into the spare room next door – Dad's sleep is very patchy and she is too worried about him to be able to get any sleep while lying next to him. She needs to be separate from him in order to care for him.

We have set up a phone line beside his bed and when he picks up the receiver a twin handset rings downstairs and we can go and see what he needs. When it rings, Mum and I will be out of our seats on the 'r' of 'ring'. We are on edge, desperate to help. In the evening when we go to bed, Mum will take the handset into her room where the bell will usually be sounded several times a night. Mum will then get up and visit Dad to help him go to the toilet or to give him the drugs that help rid him of too much pain.

I tiptoe into his room in the early morning so as not to wake him. He is fast asleep and I'm relieved that he's settled and sleeping. My own sleep is virtually non-existent at the moment. I've slept for less than two hours over the last few nights and it's beginning to show. My eyes are puffy and I feel exhausted. I have smudged a small amount of black eyeliner on my eyelids to lose some of the redness and to disguise from my mother how troubled and upset I am.

I have never shed tears like the tears I am crying alone at night for my Dad.

As I lie there in my bedroom, I think ahead to what's in store for us – the inevitable death, the funeral, a memorial service, and then, then what? I wonder to myself, what would Dad's last moment be like, how would death come to him? For the moment, there he was below me, breathing, alive. Soon he would be gone and I was dreading that day, that moment. I wanted more time with him, to speak to him and to tell him that I would make sure Mum would be alright after he had gone - I would at least promise him that.

And I also wanted to say the one thing that had always been left unsaid; I wanted to say 'I love you, Dad.'

I also wanted to thank him. Dad had done so much for me, my brother and my sister. In simply material terms, he and Mum had sacrificed a great deal. Looking back, I think they could have chosen a life of some luxury, but Dad was always insistent that education was the key to our futures and, for him, that meant paying for it. Since marrying my Mum, he'd worked in the wire industry where he had toughed it out through some difficult times to earn just enough to send us all to fee-paying schools. When it came to his job, my Dad was a real trooper, but I don't want to make him sound too conventional – in private, he showed a typical English eccentricity; not everyone goes in for snail farming as my father once did. Not everyone's garden has metal pyramids over the vegetables to help them grow bigger. Ours did. He also had a very playful side, which meant that a silly walk or a daft joke were never far away. He loved seeing us laugh and he loved to entertain. He was such a friendly soul, and I'm not looking back with rose-tinted spectacles when I say that I genuinely never heard him speak ill of anyone.

It's hard to sum up a human being in words, but my father was a really good mix of easy-going fun, intelligence and kindness.

As far as he and Mum were concerned, I rarely heard an argument. I thought this was all perfectly normal at the time but now I realise how special it was and how lucky I had been.

We had a happy and simple home life - we sat down and ate together as a family; we went on holidays in Devon or Cornwall; a trip abroad was a big treat. My parents were classic middle England - solid, honest, hard-working.

Like so many fathers and sons, Dad and I had not always got on perfectly, and there was always some degree of distance – we weren't drinking buddies, put it that way; but we nevertheless had a close, strong bond. If I look back at pictures of him in his youth, he looks just like me. There is one of him where he must be in his late thirties - about my age now - and he has his hand resting on my shoulders. We are both decked out in cricket whites and although the day is hazy to me, I can remember clearly the moment the picture was taken. We look happy and I feel happy thinking back.

My Mum says our personalities are also a close match, that I am very much alike him now, but I don't really see that. At my age, Dad had a steady job, was very sporty and was married with three kids. Compare that to me: a freelance journalist - usually unemployed - no regular partner, no kids. I spend a disproportionate amount of time going out and drinking to excess, I watch a lot of telly. We've had very different lives. But maybe Mum's right - perhaps that's why Dad and I occasionally clashed – because however disparate our lifestyles, we were, deep down, very much alike. We both tended to be quite headstrong, competitive and stubborn. I find it hard to find fault with Dad but I guess he could sometime be a bit self-righteous while I could be pig-headed, arrogant, and needlessly rebellious even though I was by now well into my thirties.

A few years ago at Christmas we had locked horns over politics – he's centre, I'm left - and on my last day at home I was stewing with frustration that he couldn't accept my way of thinking. The time came for me to leave and I wondered how this would play itself out. I looked over at Dad and he walked up to me looking sad and hurt that we had argued. He looked vulnerable and was wearing a small, tentative smile on his face. At that moment, he suddenly looked much older than I remembered. *God, why was I being such an idiot?* I hugged him and held him close and resolved there and then that I would try and work things through with him over the coming weeks. I hated the thought that I had somehow fractured our relationship. I *had* to make it better.

Thankfully, a couple of days later I did the right thing, phoned him up and apologised; and now, of course, I am so glad that I did.

But for the moment, as he lays in bed, a terminally ill man, I still worry – as perhaps many sons do – about why I had never discarded that famous English resolve, put my arms around him and told him that I loved him? Not even once! It seems ridiculous. What had stopped me and what had stopped him? Was it just a cultural thing or was it something more?

At night, as I think about all the things I have left to say to him – and I know this may seem utterly absurd - I find myself writing down a list of bullet points. I have written down *'I love you'* because these are the words I have never said to my own father and I want to tell him that I love him before it's too late. I hate to dismiss this purely as a box that I have to tick because that makes it all sound rather flippant, as if I don't really care all that much. But I care deeply. On the surface, it's no big deal and has never really bothered me before in any real, tangible sense, but now – with my father on the precipice - I feel a sense of urgency that it needs to be said and I'm a bit confused about why Dad hasn't already stepped up to the plate and said it to me.

I *must* say this to him before he dies. My father is on his way out and surely I can push all my British reservations aside for one brief moment.

I don't know why this is so important, but it is. Of course it is. Cliché or not, saying those words is a big deal to me.

Maybe the desire to say it and to hear it back is due to my own narcissistic insecurities because I know one hundred per cent that he loves me and likewise, I know that he knows that I love him. But right now, with the news that my father is dying, I'm on emotional overdrive and maybe that's why it now seems so important to open up and say these words.

I wonder if it's important for my Dad as well.

As he lies in bed below me, I can't help but feel like such an idiot that even now, now that it's important, in the last few days of his life, I can't bring myself to break the chain, go downstairs and say 'I love you, Dad.'

Whatever the reason, I want to say it to him and I want to hear it back.

My Dad, the person who is so like me, is on his way out, and Mum and I jump to attention whenever the bell goes to signify that he needs us.

We're rushing because there's not much time left.

Pop and Petal

After speaking to Mum, I head off to make the phone calls to my brother and sister that will tell them that Dad's condition is inoperable and that he is not expected to live beyond a couple of weeks.

I walk outside and up to the end of the garden where Dad has a small office. I want to do this away from Mum. I don't want her to hear me getting upset and struggling to speak. I want to be able to take time afterwards to compose myself and head back into the house to face her and tell her that Rebecca, 39, and Adam, 41, now know that their father is dying. They are aware that he is ill and has been taken to hospital for tests. They now need to be told the results.

'Rebecca,' I begin, 'I'm afraid Dad's been diagnosed with liver cancer. It's inoperable and he doesn't have long left. I think maybe you should come home when you can.'

Rebecca initially reacts by blaming the medical staff for having failed to diagnose his condition earlier, leaving it too late to save him.

'Bastards!' she cries out.

I move quickly to quell her fears on that front because I don't want mud being thrown about and Mum hasn't mentioned anything that would have suggested the hospital was at fault. I also hate the thought of getting caught up in some kind of legal entanglement. Rebecca soon calms down and asks after Mum.

'Well, she's doing OK, I think.'

But God knows how Mum really is. She seems to be managing alright but it must be so awful for her.

I call my brother too and let him know the score. We have a quick chat and I notice that my brother's voice is deep and gravelly as he checks his emotions. I too am trying to hold back from crying. The turnaround from Dad being a bit ill to having a serious illness that will kill him within weeks, maybe days, is hard to take. But Adam makes things easy for me and I am glad that I have done what needed doing and that I have saved Mum from having to make these calls.

Rebecca will be travelling up from Brighton in a day or two to join us at home. Adam is tied up at work and will be returning home at the weekend.

I sit still in Dad's office afterwards and look around me. On the walls are pictures of his parents, both of them now dead. I had been away on holiday when my grandfather, Poppa, had died and had missed the funeral. But I remember my grandmother's funeral and seeing Dad upset and in tears. And only now am I beginning to understand how he must have felt that day.

In the afternoon, Mum's younger brother David pops in to see us and it is decided that I will go up to the old people's home where my Mum's parents, Pop and Petal, are living out their last years to tell them the news about Dad's illness. They have been told that Dad is not well and that he has been in hospital but we have so far spared them the details - we don't want to frighten or alarm them with the trauma of such bad news.

I don't mind doing this at all – I'm basically up for anything that relieves any kind of burden from my mother. But I know I mustn't screw this up and I need to break the terrible news to my grandparents especially gently, to make things easy for them.

I walk up there and try to compose myself. The care home, Wheatland's, lies on top of a small hill overlooking the village and I have visited there many times before to check up on my grandparents. They have been there for nearly a year now after they were transferred from a nearby bungalow to which my Mum had moved them after life in their own home became too difficult and impractical.

They are very, very old - both of them are in their mid-nineties. My mum is 64. Will family genetics mean that she too will live to be in her nineties? Does she have another thirty years of life without Dad? Will she end up on her own in an old people's home?

I can't think about that right now, I need to focus.

I think back to when my grandparents used to live in the bungalow - there were many times when I would worry that every visit to them would be my last, that I would return to London and a few weeks later I would hear that one of them had died. But they have survived.

I remember once taking my grandfather, Pop, to hospital a few years ago. He was so old and helpless and I had to put him in a wheelchair because he was too weak to walk. As he sat down he looked up at me, put his arm on my hand and said,

'Whatever you do, don't let yourself become as old as me.'

I could have hugged him to death right there and then.

Now he is trapped in the prison of his ailing, fragile body and has no further desire for life. He has done all he wanted to do and now he doesn't really want to be alive.

And instead, my father who wanted to live and grow old with my Mum is about to die. It seems so unfair, like the wrong people have been dealt the wrong hands. Pop, I know, would have gladly swopped.

And my Mum, who had expected Hamesy to be there for her in the future, to help her through the inevitable death of her parents, will now be faced with having to endure her grief alone.

Pop is very deaf and my grandmother Petal is almost blind and we joke that together their disabilities make them the perfect couple. They have been married for over seventy years and I have never heard a cross word between them.

The last few years have not been easy for them. Their health has deteriorated considerably and they no longer have quite the same sparkle they once did. I still can't quite believe they are both still alive – I remember at least a decade before looking through their phone book and almost all the names of their friends had been crossed out, each of them having fallen by the wayside, dead and buried. Time had caught up with their friends and one day, one day soon, it would catch up with them too.

When visiting them I would sometimes think that this could be the last time I would ever see them. A few years ago when I once went to see them at their bungalow, I looked at them and they seemed so frail, so weak, that it didn't seem possible that they could live much longer. After I had told them my news I got up to leave, looked at them and just like I was struggling right now with telling my own father that I loved him, I wanted to tell them, for the first time, that I loved them.

'OK you two, I'd better be on my way. I love you lots, see you both soon.'

Without really thinking about it too much, I'd said it. No agonising, no problem. I perhaps hadn't said it as directly as I would have wanted; it wasn't an 'I love you Pop, I love you Petal.' Instead, it was hidden in a goodbye, but for me, and I hope for them, it was enough.

'Goodbye Darling,' Petal replied.

I didn't mind that there was no 'I love you,' said back to me. Petal and Pop were of a very different generation where I think feelings and emotions were kept to oneself. In their day, there was certain decorum, and certain things that were best left unsaid. I could have no complaints – as grandparents I couldn't have hoped for better. They were always supportive, kind and affectionate, without being soppy. But sure, they both had something of the English stiff upper lip about them. And that was fair enough really.

I suppose the same applies for my more immediate family. I've never considered us particularly uptight; on the whole, I'd say we're a pretty open and honest family, but we haven't ever felt the need to go all gooey and lovey-dovey towards each other. Besides, if you say 'I love you' too many times, doesn't that render it a bit meaningless? Say it once and it means everything.

But saying these words can be cathartic and I definitely felt better for having told Petal and Pop that I loved them. There was a weight lifted as I walked away from their bungalow and down the driveway. I looked behind me to wave goodbye to Pop before I turned the corner. He was stood at the doorway of their conservatory smiling and waving. To his right, I caught a glimpse of Petal who was sat in her armchair with her back to me. I saw she was struggling to lift her arm and waited a moment. She finally managed to raise her arm was and I saw her hand motion slowly from side to side. I waved back and then made my way back home hoping to hide my tears before anyone noticed.

Nowadays, in the care home, my grandparents' time consists largely of recovering from the hassle of having to get up in the morning and being moved to and from the dining room for food. Pop still reads the newspaper and they listen to and watch the television for an hour or two in the evening. At this stage in their lives both are still mentally with it, surprisingly so, but we are still very concerned about how they will take this news and we have warned the carers that I will be telling them about Dad later that day.

I knock on the door of their room and walk in. As soon as I appear, Pop reaches out a hand to me and I can see that just having seen me he is already on the verge of tears. I clasp his hand and kiss him hello.

Pop is crying now but he cries a lot in his old age and I am not unduly worried by it so I quietly tell him not to cry and to settle, to calm down, that everything will be alright. Then I move over to Petal who sits in the chair beside him. She is a tiny hunched up figure, her head bowed low, but although her sight has gone she is very much alive and aware of everything going on around her. Something tells me that she already knows what I am here to say.

I sit down on the bed opposite them as Pop struggles to adjust his hearing aid.

'How's your father?' Petal asks me.

'Not good, I'm afraid. I've come here to tell you some bad news.'

I look down at the floor and then back up at Pop and Petal and I can't bear the fact that this is happening. My eyes well up and my voice falters. A couple of tears slip down my face.

'Take your time,' I hear Petal say quietly to me.

I am hugely encouraged to hear these words and take immense strength from them. This means they are thinking and cogent; they are not panicking. I pull myself together and tell them the details of how ill Dad is, and that it's unlikely that he will live for very much longer.

Pop has understood, but as I continue talking I can see that he is having trouble hearing me. This isn't the kind of conversation I want to have to shout across the room at him so I begin to write down what is happening back at home and pass him the notes that I hope will reassure him that his daughter, my mother, is managing alright. This isn't a lie – I think Mum is managing as well as could possibly be expected. But there's no means for me to possibly express how I think she's really feeling; this has hit Mum hard - she's sad and upset beyond words - but I still want to protect her parents from too much heartbreak.

For Pop, I write down that *'Mum is OK, but I need you to understand that she is very upset and I need you to be strong for her.'* Pop nods and has understood, but I have only really scratched the surface. Nonetheless, I think that's probably enough information for them now – I'm concerned that any more emotional blows could tip them over the edge and into an unnecessarily distressed state.

Mum hasn't been up to see them for several days now and as she usually visited them every day without fail, I suspect that this had already alerted them to the fact there was something seriously wrong back at home. Whatever their suspicions, I am glad that I have managed to tell them about Dad and that they have been put in the picture. Pop begins to cry again and I hold his arm and tell him that we will be alright, that we'll get through this. And then I leave them and go and tell one of the carers that they now know the situation and that she should check up on them shortly to make sure that they are alright.

India

I tell Dad that Rebecca – my elder sister - is coming up tomorrow to stay with us and he smiles back at me: he's happy about that. Any tiny glimmer of happiness that comes from him makes me feel, for an instant, utterly joyful. At the moment, my emotions are pitched at extremes, there is no middle ground. Other people have been asking to see Dad but we are screening him from seeing too many people. He is tiring easily now and I want him to save his energy for Mum. I want him to spend as much time with Mum as possible and I speak to her about this because I am keenly aware that time is running out for them. But she knows this; Mum is right at the sharp end and is there for Dad every second of the day.

I have texted some friends to let them know that I won't be around for a while because of my Dad's illness. I get some really supportive texts back from them and I feel glad for that. A bit selfishly, I want some reassurance that I am wanted, missed, and liked, and I get all that and more. One of the messages is from an ex-girlfriend who had been one of the great loves of my life – India.

The first time I saw India I was sat opposite her on a train journey back to London having been away for a weekend with Mum and Dad in Shropshire. I had plonked myself down in a seat and there, across from me, was this incredibly beautiful creature. God, I so wanted to talk to her! But as I'm all too aware, I sometimes find it hard to express myself. Would this be another opportunity lost?

I was wearing dark sunglasses and used them to turn my head towards the window while looking straight at her. I was mesmerised. Sweet blue eyes, chaotic blond hair: perfection.

Right, I have to speak to this girl before I get to London or else I am really going to regret this. True to form though, I couldn't get a sentence out. I sat for a while, not a word, and then, an hour or so later, we had to change trains somewhere down the line. I got out and watched this lovely girl standing near me on the platform. I then watched her get on the next train to London and purposely got on a different carriage so I wouldn't have to deal with the tension of wanting but being unable to speak to her.

I sat down and before long she walked past me on the train and returned a few minutes later clasping a drink.

God she moves so well.

OK, that's it, if I see her on the platform when we get to London I am going to HAVE to speak to her. If I don't, then it wasn't meant to be.

There I go again, leaving it all in the hands of fate and taking no personal responsibility. *Yeah, that'll work. Christ, I'm such a dork.*

The train arrives at Euston station and I'm praying I bump into her on my way out. But there's no sign of her. *Dammit!* I'd screwed up. Again.

I don't want to get on the tube straight away – I feel too frustrated, stressed out and annoyed at myself for being so weak. I feel like such a dork. I need a cigarette and head outside. And blimey, there she is, sitting on a bench. *Wow. She's gorgeous.* I walk towards her but again I know I am going to blow it and shy away from talking to her yet again so I carry on walking. But just as I move past her I hear a voice pipe up:

'Do you have a lighter please?'

Brilliant. She just saved me.

'Sure. Here you go.'

I hand her my lighter and get a cigarette out for myself.

'Sorry I didn't speak to you on the train. I thought you were so beautiful and I just couldn't say anything.'

Christ, did I really just say that?

She smiles and looks up at me.

'Thank-you.'

'Are you a model or something?'

Geez, I am really cheesing this one up, but I can't help it.

'No, I'm a student.'

'Oh, OK. You could so easily be a model you know.'

Oh for fuck's sake!

'What about you, what do you do then?'

I tell her I work in television and then ask her how old she is.

She is only 18. I thought she was at least 22, 23, so I'm a bit taken aback - eighteen seems a bit young for someone like me in his early thirties. Ah, whatever, I think, let's do this.

'Listen, do you fancy going out for a drink sometime?'

'Sure.'

And that was how my love affair with India began. It had taken me just minutes to fall for her and it was only another two weeks before I met up with her in a pub, had a few drinks and some games of pool and then pulled her towards me:

'I love you, India.'

India's eyes sparkled.

'You know, you don't have to say it back to me, I just want you to know that I really do love you.'

And God did I love that girl. Everything before India now made perfect sense. Somehow she validated all my previous experiences because now they all added up to this moment, to me meeting her and to us falling in love. And I knew India loved me, of that I was later left in no doubt. I remember her once looking down at my naked body and saying out loud in mock frustration:

'Arrgh, I want to EAT you!'

And when she spoke those words, I remember at the time that Dad had told us the same - that when me, my brother and my sister were babies, we smelt so nice that we seemed almost edible.

And right now that's how I thought about India too: yummy.

But saying 'I love you' to your girlfriend is different to saying it to your Dad, isn't it? With your girlfriend it's about being 'in love' as well as just loving. It's about romance and somehow it's just so much easier. With a partner too, it's more obvious: that moment when you fall in love, you can feel it in the pit of your stomach, and when you feel it with a passion you can't help yourself from blurting it out.

But it seems odd that you can say these words to someone who you've perhaps known for only a matter of weeks or months yet deny yourself the pleasure of saying it to someone who you've known and been super-close to for your entire life. When I think of my father now, I know I have and always will have a deeper connection with him than possibly with anyone else. He's my Dad, that's normal. But was it normal that neither of us had felt the right moment to face up to each other, to perhaps show some emotional vulnerability and to say 'I love you?'

Why should this little sentence be such a big stumbling block?

It's not a macho thing – Dad and I are both softies at heart. Perhaps it's generational, with people of my father's age being more inclined to keep a lid on their emotions, whereas I'm usually more inclined to say whatever's on my mind. Or perhaps it's a bit like knowing someone for ages but never learning their name - after a while, you finally reach a point of no-return where it becomes just too big a deal, too much of an embarrassment. Dad and I went past that point a long time ago.

For the moment, it is left unsaid and we remain the classic middle-class English family – a bit repressed.

A month after I first told India that I loved her, we sat down together for a greasy fry-up in my local cafe. I looked across at her and felt an overwhelming urge to ask her to marry me. Only the fact that she was so young did I resist. It was unfair to expect an eighteen year old to commit for a lifetime. It didn't seem fair. I knew India loved me – by now she'd told me - and I knew she wanted to be with me but maybe this was a step too far and perhaps a bit too soon. I hesitated, said nothing, pulled out the newspaper and handed India the salt.

Another six months down the line and India and I had had the first of many break-ups, eventually leading to a permanent separation. And now back at home with my Mum and Dad - some three years and a lot of tears later - I hungered to see her again. In the face of crisis, everything had reduced and pulled into focus. I wanted someone close to me and I wanted India to be by my side. I was also eager to speak to someone outside of my immediate family. I felt like I needed to off-load a little but also to talk about something other than the unhappiness that had arrived on our doorstep in the shape of my father's illness.

I go downstairs and speak to Mum and ask her if she minds India coming up for a quick visit. Mum thinks that's a great idea saying that India could help lift our spirits a little. She's right and I instantly can't stop smiling at the thought that India is on her way to see us. When she arrives and I open the door to her it's the first time I have seen her for about a year and she looks so fresh and young and lively. It's great to see her again and I pull her towards me and she smells adorable and I remember that smell so well and it makes me love her instantly all over again. I invite her in and Mum comes over, gives her a hug and then puts a brew on.

While India and Mum have a little catch up I walk upstairs to see Dad to ask if he'd like India to come up and say hello. He is sound asleep which is nice to see, so I go back downstairs and India and I decide to go for a walk. It's cold outside so we get wrapped up and then head off down the road together. Just twenty yards away we see an ambulance parked up outside the house of one of the neighbours. This is where my Mum's friend Norma lives with her husband. As we walk past the ambulance together I throw out a jokey remark to India:

'Bloody hell, they're falling like flies here in Much Wenlock.'

Just a day later I find out that my words had rung horribly true. After returning from holiday that afternoon, Norma had gone to the kitchen to make her husband a cup of tea and returned just minutes later to find him dead in his chair. He had suffered a massive heart attack and had died on the spot.

One second he is there and the next, he is not.

At least *we* have been given time to say our goodbyes. Norma has not been so lucky.

Nor, sadly, will India. When we return, my father is still sound asleep and he doesn't stir for the rest of the day. India has to drive back to London that evening and though I ask her to stay the night she decides to make her way back down South. She has a new boyfriend; it wouldn't be right. I didn't know she was seeing someone else but I don't feel bad about it; it's fine. She won't be able to say her farewells to my father but I think perhaps that's a good thing – she still seems really young and I think it's best she doesn't have to deal with a traumatic, final goodbye. Dad thought she was a cracking girl but it will be enough for him to know that she has been to pay us all a visit.

I feel re-energised by India's presence and so glad that she wanted to come up and lend her support. It means a lot to me and I thank her for coming. I hope it is not so long before we can meet up again but gradually time will pass, moments come and go, and then it will be more than a year before I see her again.

Smoking

Since Dad's death, I've found that my own mortality has, not surprisingly, come into even sharper focus. I am now 37. If I die at the same age as my father, I am already well past the half-way mark. I wonder how I might die?

Maybe a car crash?
Parkinsons?
Alzheimers?

Christ, all these bloody nightmares that lie in wait.

Maybe I'll eventually top myself to avoid all these agonies. And how would I go about that – maybe I'll do a Kurt Cobain and blow my brains out with a gun. Perhaps I could jump in front of a train or rig up the car exhaust pipe. In my darker moments, I've given it some thought. But the likelihood, of course, is that I will die, like my father, from cancer. In fact, my lifestyle pretty much dictates that lung, throat or stomach cancer will be the end of me. I mean, it's getting to the point now where cigarettes are an almost constant companion for me. It's utterly bizarre: at the very time when I am trying to cope with the death of my father from cancer, it is a carcinogenic, cancer-inducing drug that seems to be providing me with the most solace.

Cigarettes are my crutch, and I'm grateful for them: when I feel upset I don't reach for the lettuce, tomato or cucumber – salad just doesn't do the trick for me. No, I turn instead to the cigarette. Suck on that Sunshine, breathe in deeply and try to relax. Heck, it even works sometimes, makes me feel better, more focussed and more alert to the here and now rather than dwelling on what's happened in the past. Or flip that and use cigarettes to reminisce and reflect – they can help you do that too. Cigarettes are multi-purpose; the only trouble is that they will surely lead to my early death – but then I wonder: Is that really a problem? Do I actually want to get to the same age and condition as my grandparents? Well, no disrespect, but no thanks. Anyhow, I'm guessing that my smoking habit is a sure-fire guarantee that that won't happen. Even if I gave up now I must already have done irreparable damage. But so what? – Taking the healthy option didn't exactly help my Dad did it?

My smoking has got way out of hand since Dad died. It's got to farcical proportions where I will start to worry about the fact that I'm smoking so much and reach for a cigarette to try and ease my anxiety. That's some circle.

Mind you, it's hardly heroin is it? When my sister calls on the phone me some time after Dad has died to see if I'm alright and asks me if I'm still smoking, then that's my back-up - I explain to her that I allow myself just the one addiction – I seldom, if ever, do drugs anymore, so cigarettes have to stay. I have to have *something*. Besides, I'm starting to accept that perhaps this way of life is my own particular form of suicide. Screw the bullet and the trigger – I'm using cigarettes and alcohol – at least it's more fun this way.

At the moment, I'm on at least twenty-five, thirty a day and have been smoking regularly for the past 17 or 18 years. And it's more like forty a day if I'm sat at home writing, like now. Before the UK's smoking ban in pubs I would neck at least fifty fags on a night out, probably nearer 60. I never used to smoke in the morning but that's now changed. Before my Dad died I would have a kick off point – first off it was 3 pm. That was later amended to lunchtime. Now, I have two cigarettes while I'm running the bath first thing in the morning. Then a couple afterwards while the sausages burn in the oven. I'll have done ten before lunch unless I'm having an off-day.

Basically, I think we're on safe ground to say that I smoke like a freakin' maniac; sometimes I only eat because I know the cigarette tastes nicer afterwards. Even then, what I eat is cheap and nasty – heart-attack-friendly fry-ups or insta-cook microwave meals. If they made your daily recommended dose of food into a pill, I'd take it and ditch food altogether. Just give me a cigarette and a cold Diet Coke – that's heaven to me….even if it's bringing me ever closer to an early grave. Mind you, looking on the bright side - provided there really is a heaven and with the proviso that I actually make it in, it's not *such* a vicious circle. Why hang around on earth if the glories of heaven are waiting for you? As things stand though, that is quite a big 'if.'

I'm wondering now just how many ciggies I've actually smoked across my entire lifetime – oh boy, even *I'm* dreading the results of this calculation. But if we work it out, conservatively, as say, twenty a day for 20 years, we get a round figure of 150,000 cigarettes. My guess is that it's probably even more. That's totally *insane*! Add in thousands, *thousands* of pints of lager, hundreds of bottles of vodka, shot after shot of San Buca, a few bags of weed and one big spade-full of cocaine and I'm starting to think I'm actually still quite lucky to be alive.

They say that cigarettes help to age you prematurely. I don't reckon I look all that bad but sure, I've deteriorated quite rapidly over the last year or two and I sense that things are moving on quite fast now.

I look in the mirror and I hate the signs of aging – the middle-aged spread of an expanding waistline, a slightly receding hairline, some wrinkles around the eyes, muscles going to waste. I'm doing *nothing* to combat the deterioration of my physical well-being – I have done *no* exercise for about three years. They say the elderly tend to pass their days in an armchair watching TV all day as the world passes by outside. Hmm, that sounds horribly familiar already.

I do literally *zero* to keep myself in shape. Press-ups? Sit-ups? Go for a run? Forget it. The limit of my daily physical exertion is walking a hundred yards to my local corner-shop to buy a packet of cigarettes, some coke, crisps and the newspaper. My breasts are starting to droop a little – and I'm a man! These days, I can scarcely last more than ten minutes in the sack – not because I'm done and dusted but because I've run out of breath. I can hear my lungs rasping with breath as they struggle to keep up with me. Seriously, it's embarrassing.

I wonder what this all means for my life expectancy. I recently did a *'When Will You Die?'* test on the Internet and that came up with the figure of 74 years old. I think that's wildly optimistic. As things stand, I think I'll probably die in my late forties, early fifties. Jesus.

And who will be there for me when I finally go? Will I have a wife and a son or a daughter at my side? Will my Mum be there for me like she was for Dad? Will she have to endure further agony on my behalf? Will my brother and sister be beside me as I suffer my last moments in the ward of some non-descript hospital ward? Will it come suddenly and will I be conscious when the final moment arrives?

Or will I die in my sleep?

I've already had one close-call on that front – 17 years old, gallons of newly-discovered alcohol down my neck, waking up at a friend's house with sick all over the sheets: I'd slept through it. To think, if I'd fallen unconscious on my back and not on my front, I doubt I'd be writing this right now: such a miniscule difference, one twist of fate, means I'm still breathing rather than being discovered in the morning as a teenage casualty who has choked to death on his own vomit. Amazing to think that such tiny nuances are what divide the living from the dead. Some of us are lucky, and some of us...aren't.

I know there are those who say there's nothing to be afraid of – that death is just a fact of life. But that hardly makes it any easier does it? And are we *really* thinking about it all that much? I'm absolutely *petrified* of dying. Here I am, coasting along through life and then bang! – Nothing. It's all going to end. Boom! – It's over. And none of us know how, when or where it's going to happen.

And I guess the 'Boom! - It's over' scenario is the best of all the options rather than a ground-out long-term dose of suffering. Much as I love them, I dread to think of myself getting to the same point as my grandparents – I simply don't want to become so old that I am physically unable to carry out the decision to end my own life. I can't bear the thought of being hoisted into a wheelchair and pushed around by some poorly-paid care worker. I don't want to be a burden to anyone – not my family, not the NHS, no-one. I just want to live a little bit and then knock it all on the head while I still can.

I think back to one time when I saw my grandfather Pop up in the care home. I remember him reaching towards my Mum, taking her arm and pulling her over towards him.

'I didn't mean...to...last...this long,' he said, in between quiet, gentle sobs.

He doesn't need to apologise.

I remember back to when I was a child and my Mum pinching up the loose skin on the back of her hand – she is showing me how it delays settling back to the surface because she says she has the hands of an old lady. Back then my skin was taught and it would spring back. Now, it is more like my mother's.

But then I think of how I also love getting older and the knowledge, ease and confidence, the earthiness and grit that comes with age. I love the fact that when you're 20, you look back to when you were in your teens and you think, 'what an idiot I was back then.' And I love the fact that when you're 30, you look back at when you were 20 and you think, 'what an idiot I was back then.' And I know, or at least hope, that I will love it when I am 40 and 50 for exactly the same reason.

And yet I selfishly hate the fact that the world won't stop for me when I die. It won't stop for my father and it won't stop for me or for anyone else. Annoyingly, yet, I have to admit, quite brilliantly, life carries on and the world keeps turning. I think of a few exceptional historic figures – Einstein, Van Gogh, Mozart…George Best – and wish that I too could leave an indelible mark on society and be remembered; but the overwhelming likelihood is that I won't. Very few people ever will. But does it really matter anyway when you're not around to enjoy your own immortality? At least death makes us all equal - when the crunch comes, we're all just as insignificant as each other.

Sometimes, it feels like life is just one endless gathering in a big living room. You make your entrance, say 'hi' to a few people, enjoy a few nibbles, and just when you've got to know and work out who you want to be with and where you want to hang out, it's time to leave. As you make your way out of the revolving door, others – fresh blood - are waiting to get inside and replace you. You'll be missed, but not that much. Minutes later, the conversation has changed and what you were saying, what interested you, what you invested your time in and what was important when you had your moment is now irrelevant, forgotten. History just doesn't care.

It's weird: I could never have conceived that I would one day be the oldest bloke at the bar in my local pub. Today, newer, younger, fresher faces have taken over. When I go for a drink and look around me I can see people who are like I once was – fresh and enthusiastic, with good hair. I have seen seven landlords work there and move on since I ordered my first pint. I have met and spoken to countless bar staff, all of them just passing through. The clientele is like it always was – young twenty-somethings flirting with hope and ambition, wanting to get laid. In my head I still feel carefree, and I still feel like I could party with the best of them, but I know that my body isn't what it once was. Drink too much in your twenties and you're irresponsible; drink too much at my age and you're labelled as sad.

Only now, in my thirties, do I really understand the old cliché that time really is precious, and that time truly does fly. I would never have imagined that I would ever be the same age as say, today's leading political figures. Now, government ministers are the same age as me, which, as a perennial teenager at heart, I find utterly bizarre. I even think I would feel comfortable having a pint down the boozer with Barack Obama – how weird is that? We now have a US President who is pretty much of my own generation, with similar life experiences to me. How did that happen? I got older, that's what happened.

Today, I have an acute sense that my time has gone – I'm not part of the zeitgeist any more - I feel irrelevant and out of touch, disconnected and detached. It seems like my life is over when I'd really only just got started. I'm not even 40 yet and it already seems like I'm a spent force, at the exact time when I feel like my brain is at last a fully-formed and well-functioning entity.

Rewind to the 1990's and I felt like I was in the eye of the storm, at the centre of my own particular universe, with endless possibilities and limitless potential. I was excited by the world around me, I felt like exploring and going out, I was hungry to meet people and let loose. Now, I just want to stay at home and relax and hope that there's no post that day and that I'm not hassled by anyone on the phone. I don't want to go out any more, I don't want to make any new friends, I don't want to see what's out there; I'm simply not interested.

Now, I'm just part of the background, I'm no longer relevant, I simply *exist*.

If I go away and come back from a few months abroad, it's noticeable how the people I see on television have aged in my absence – Barack Obama's hair has grown greyer, newsreaders look a little more tired. Due to the fact that I see myself every day in the mirror I don't notice those physical changes in myself – but as sure as mustard, I too will have changed, I have grown older, and I am a step nearer death.

Humans are a bit like computers – we start off functioning efficiently and then we hit a sell-by-date and things begin to fall apart. Eventually we just fizzle out and we can't be re-booted. We're just used up, scrap metal, gone forever. There can be no doubts: we all have a shelf-life and one day we'll all end up on the rubbish tip of history.

If I didn't see it before, then Dad's own death has made me see that there really is, undeniably, a finish line. I can clearly make out the horizon, and that scares me but also invigorates me – I feel the urge to get my act together and make the best use of my time. Before he died, my dad was planning on writing a book aimed at people of retirement age; it was to be a self-help book about making the most of the last ten or twenty years of your life and he had called it 'What Are You Going To Do With The Rest Of Your Life? Now, with all the clarity in the world, I can see that's a valid question for any person of any age. For all I know, my heart could stop beating tomorrow – and to think I must have spent something like half of the past ten years either drunk or slumped in front of the telly. Mind you, who's to say that all that time watching trash TV or slamming back the beers has been wasted rather than well spent? I suppose I have to be the judge of that and sure, to be honest, my gut tells me I could have made some better decisions.

For sure, Dad has been a far better person than me, and in the days to come, I will try to reassure him that if there is a God and if there is any fairness in the world, then his place at the Top Table is a sure-fire guarantee. And he will smile and tell me he's not concerned about that. I wish I could be so confident, but it's true: he really has nothing to be scared of on that front.

I will also smile and in the interests of continuing the slightly debauched bachelor lifestyle to which I have become accustomed, I will ask that if he does get the opportunity to look down on me from the clouds, that I apologise in advance if my behaviour is sometimes a bit sinful on occasion.

And he will look at me and say, *'I know, don't you worry about that.'*

Mum says that before Dad was diagnosed with cancer she had not even remotely contemplated the possibility of him dying. And she had no real reason to - Dad was something of a health freak, an organic gardener before it became trendy. About five or six years ago as they entered their sixties, they had bought the house where my Mum now lives – this, they both assumed, was the place where they would grow old together.

I enjoyed going back there to visit them and a few months before my Dad became ill, I had travelled up from London to be with my parents.

We were at the top of the garden together and I got out my camera phone to take a picture of Mum and Dad. I beckoned them to stand together in front of the house with which they had both fallen in love. Dad put his arm around my Mum and I took a picture. I wasn't quite satisfied with it because Dad had a baseball cap on and looked a bit silly and Mum didn't look quite right either. I told Dad to sort his headwear out and he messed around with me and ended up putting on two hats. I asked Mum to smile. I framed the picture up: they looked great together and I took the shot. I looked back at it and said I was happy with it and let them get on with their gardening. But I was struck by the thought that the picture was just too perfect and part of me somewhere deep down worried that it would be the last ever picture I would ever take of them together.

And I don't know why I thought that, but I did.

When I returned to London, I thought of sending the picture back to them but wanted to keep it just for myself. I framed it up and it has been hanging on the wall of my flat ever since.

DAY THREE

Rebecca

Morning comes and after an early drive up from Brighton, my sister Rebecca arrives with her boyfriend, Richard. At first it will seem strange having her there. The atmosphere, the dynamic will change: Mum and I had been alone with Dad and we were growing together as a team. We needed each other and were helping each other.

I don't want that spell to be broken.

I go outside to greet Rebecca.

'Hi Boo,' I say as she steps out of the car. She already looks strained and upset.

'How's Dad?' she asks.

'He's OK, you know. He seems fine with everything.'

She looks at me and I can sense myself struggling with my words.

'He looks a bit like Poppa,' I say.

Poppa was my father's Dad.

'When you go and see him you may get upset.'

As I say these words my face contorts with grief and tears start falling from my eyes. I am struggling for breath and heave air in and out. And then, just as suddenly, my body recovers itself and I am able to continue.

'But then that moment will pass - just like with me now - and you'll be fine. Just let it happen.'

We walk inside and she goes up to see Dad. I can hear her laughing with him but I feel like it's shot through with confusion and anxiety. When I walk past Dad's bedroom I see Rebecca sitting on a chair next to the bed and our eyes meet for an instant as I go upstairs. I don't know why but I start to worry that she isn't letting the full impact of his illness affect her. I sense this even more strongly later on during the day and it starts eating away at me. I'm concerned that she hasn't fully grasped what's going on but I know it's just her mind putting up a barrier, a defence mechanism to protect her from facing a truth too dreadful for her to contemplate. I don't think it's my place to confront her in order to try and get her to register the truth as I see it, but it nags away at me and I decide to have a quick word with Mum.

'Mum, what do you think about Rebecca? I don't want to put a spanner in the works, but I'm not sure she's really registered that Dad…that Dad's about to die.'

I see Mum nodding in quiet agreement.

'What do you think? Should I say anything?'

'I know what you mean,' Mum answers.

She has sensed that something is amiss too.

'But we'll all deal with our grief in different ways,' she continues. 'She'll come to terms with it when she's good and ready. Don't say anything yet.'

Mum's right and I agree that I'll keep a lid on what I'm thinking. Later that evening however, I start to nudge my sister. Whatever Mum has said, I can't help myself. I feel like Rebecca has missed out on the build-up to Dad's imminent departure. I have been lucky enough to have been at home with Mum, working through the puzzle in my mind. I want to help Rebecca catch up with us and get past what I think is essentially a state of denial. I think she was expecting Dad to be walking around, having supper with us, and watching television. But things are far from normal on the home front: Dad is bedridden.

I ask her how she feels about Dad and she immediately admits to me that she is struggling to come to terms with what is happening right now - that her father is dying and that he won't be around much longer. She says it just seems like he's a bit ill but that he's not really going to die.

I don't push it any further and let things rest.

Later, Rebecca's boyfriend leaves and we are down to the four of us – my Mum and my sister, Dad and I. My brother, Adam, has been on the phone and is coming to stay for the weekend.

I am still keen to try and help Rebecca to get a handle on Dad's situation – I can sense a strange tension in the air and, without saying anything to me, I now feel that Mum may want me to have words with my sister. I could be wrong but I'm willing to trust my instincts. We sit down together and again I broach the subject of how she is feeling and try to push her towards the harsh facts, towards acceptance. I'm stating the obvious but I warn her explicitly that time is running out and that she needs to be able to say all the things to Dad that she wants to while she still has the opportunity. Like me, I want her to use the little time we have left with Dad to tell him that she loves him. I want everything to be said; I don't want anyone to have any regrets.

'I don't think Dad will live for very much longer. You do realise that don't you? He may even have as little as a few days left.'

Rebecca looks at me silently. But she leans forward and I think she wants me to continue.

'I just want you to try and get your head round this as soon as you can, you know. While he's here you can say anything you want to him and he'll be there to listen to you.'

Rebecca is nodding and I know that she understands I am trying to help her rather than just being an irritating, patronising younger brother. I think in some ways I am also trying to help myself here: I still desperately want to go to Dad's bedside and tell him that I love him and I am all too aware and frustrated with myself that I still haven't done that yet. The fact that I haven't is starting to gnaw away at me. With my father so ill, yet still alive, I realise how lucky I am to have the opportunity that so many others miss out on. I didn't want to blow my chance, I don't want things left hanging; I don't want to be left as one of those sons who had never got the chance to say…

Neither do I want Rebecca to have the same regret that I fear may leave me feeling haunted. I decide to go for some kind of hammer blow to push things forward.

'Listen Rebecca, it's not just you: we all need to get to grips with this. In just a couple of weeks all that will be left of Dad will be a gravestone in a church yard with his name on it.'

I hate saying these words to her and I surprise myself by talking in such a straightforward, blunt manner, but I am glad afterwards that I did because I see Rebecca nodding at me as she says, 'I know, Ash. I know.'

Straight away, I feel the air has been cleared and within a few hours I feel way more confident that a flip-switch in Rebecca has been tripped: she is starting to face reality. Also, there seems to be a more peaceful, tranquil atmosphere. By the evening, after seeing her talking more with Mum and Dad, I'm really happy that we spoke: she's spending more and more time with Dad and now I'm sensing that we're all on the same track.

Cheer Up

Today, walking down to the tube station in London I hear a man's voice call out to me: 'Cheer up!' he says.

I look behind me as he passes by. He's smiling at me with encouragement and I face towards him and force a smile back at him but carry on walking. I don't want any further contact - he's not anyone I know, just a complete stranger who simply walks past me in the street. As I head down the steps towards the station I'm angered that anyone would even care to point out the truth to me – that I apparently look visibly depressed. But although I'm sure he had the best intentions, it's hardly a comment that is going to put my world back together, is it? If anything, it makes me feel even worse, even more acutely aware of how things have changed since the death of my father.

I'm surprised though - I didn't think my depressed state of mind actually showed up on the outside. I'm not walking around in tears or anything, but I quite plainly don't look happy. Still, I have every right to be a bit depressed without being pulled up about it, don't I?

Then again, maybe this stranger is right – that I should get my act together, stop being so self-absorbed and reach for a brighter outlook on life.

I'm increasingly worried that I'm starting to look upset all the time because this is, in fact, not an isolated incident. Just two weeks before, I had gone to my local supermarket where one of the security guards actually called me over as I walked through the entrance:

'Excuse me; I see you coming here a lot – but tell me, why do you always look so pissed off?'

I couldn't believe what I was hearing. *If I am pissed off*, I thought, *is it any of your business? Besides, do you really want to know?*

I said nothing, forced myself into raising a grin and said, 'Oh, I don't know. Thanks for asking though.'

Jesus! Leave me alone! I feel like even more of a bad-tempered bastard now, thanks very much.

I wonder though, do I really have a face like thunder? I wasn't aware that looking so hacked off had become my natural state of being. That's worrying. And I'm amazed that my mood is so obviously visible to complete strangers. And that they would feel so moved to comment. This, after all, is England, where people leave other people alone, where important, sensitive things are left unsaid.

When I get back to my flat I start to think even worse thoughts – that my demeanour, my physical look, is actually starting to bear the impact of losing my father. I'm really worried about this – about changing, morphing into a new, sadder version of my former self. I used to be so ready with a smile, eager to please, chilled out, relaxed and generally very happy. I've been so spoilt, so lucky, and now life – well, death - has jumped in foot-first and changed everything.

It was never normal for me to appear dejected and sad. Have I changed forever? Is my face really starting to tell the story of my family's recent past? Will I recover my previous happy self or is this it? It's not like I'm wearing black and weeping constantly in public, but something, *something* about me has changed. I don't mean to look miserable or depressed but maybe I do - at least it seems like that's the case – and that really concerns me.

Will I ever get back to how I was before, or is this a wound that will never heal? I'm beginning to suspect so.

Christ I feel like I'm reflecting in my writing what I'm apparently showing on my face – I'm moaning here on this piece of paper and I hate moaning, I hate being self-absorbed. I hate rattling over the same old material. I think I need to sort my life out, break things down into basics:

My Dad is dead.
It happens to everyone.
You're a grown man.
Get over it.

Problem is, whatever I say, whatever methods I try to use, I'm overcome with the conviction that the death of a parent is something you don't actually ever get over. Instead, I just think it's something you live with, something that's with you forever. And I'm sure this will be the same for Mum.

After Dad has died, Mum tells me that she had attended a meeting of the local council. There she had been introduced to a widow who lives nearby and who had heard about my mother's loss.

'It doesn't get any better, you know,' she told my Mum.

Not the best thing for my Mum to hear. But inside I'm worried that this lady is right – it really doesn't get any better.

I still find myself constantly mulling over my Dad's final moments and it makes me feel winded, like a part of my soul has just escaped from me. There are days when I will be walking home and feel absolutely fine, not a care in the world, and then suddenly I will think back to my father breathing his last breaths and I will slow down and a combination of dread and intense sadness will sweep over me.

I think I must have been traumatised or something. It's like some kind of shell-shock.

At night time I will be lying in bed reading a book, then lean over to turn off the light and as I do I find myself suddenly transported back to my father's bedside as he struggles to stay alive and so I keep the light on and wait until the moment passes. It's a feeling of dread and torture; it's the finality of it all that I struggle to get my head around; it's nausea fused with an intense sense of isolation and loneliness.

The Skeleton

I live alone in my flat in South London and today I have said one sentence out loud all day:
'Twenty Marlboro Lights please.'
Christ! I need to get out more. This whole being-alone-in-my-flat-all-day-and-not-working thing really isn't good for me: too much time to think. This is nothing new - I've lived on my own for years now, nearly ten years, but more recently I can feel myself becoming more and more of a recluse. I'm not sure if that's related to what's happened back home in Shropshire or not, but maybe it's something I need to think about changing...it's starting to feel really unhealthy.
For now though, I can't get back to sleep for a while because the hollow pain of loss is lingering. Again I think of my Dad's final moments and I'm fully awake once more and it feels like a small but irreplaceable part of my spirit has just been ripped from my body.
I am starting to truly regret that I was there for Dad's last moments – I wish now that I hadn't been there and that instead, I had, like my father had suggested, saved my last memories of him for whilst he was alive. But it's too late now – what's done is done, and all I can do is read some more and smoke another few cigarettes until the early hours until finally I am asleep.
I am so close to tears at every moment it's ridiculous – It's like my heart strings have been exhumed and placed on the surface of my chest –

nowadays, I'm such a pushover it's unreal. Christ, I'm becoming more like my granddad with every passing day. Thinking about it, that's not such a bad thing – he's a lovely man, but he still cries relentlessly whenever I go back to visit him. The only difference these days is that I'm just as likely to join in with the waterworks. We make a good couple.

I always ask Mum on the phone how my grandparents are – they are as well as could be expected but to be honest, that's no great shakes. Mum says that Pop has recently spoken to her about my grandmother Petal, about expecting one day to wake up and find her no longer at the breakfast table because she will have died in the night. I am so glad that my granddad is at least expressing his fears and preparing himself for the inevitable: it is plain for everyone to see that Petal, his wife of more than seventy years, is perilously close to the end of her life. But I am also sad because I know Mum doesn't really impose her own grief and suffering about Dad onto her parents because they already have a lot on their plate just by struggling through their day-to-day existence.

I went to see them recently at the old people's home where they live: Pop was sitting in his chair, with Petal - as ever - beside him in their room, asleep. Pop lifted his arm up to greet me as I entered and I walked over and kissed him hello.

Petal doesn't stir – she has a bandage on her leg because a couple of days earlier, she needed to go to the toilet and Pop had tried to help her up but she had fallen and hurt herself. Neither of them can walk unassisted any more.

I have words with Pop telling him that he must use the red button next to his bed to call for help from a care worker the next time either of them need anything. I know Mum has told him this already but Pop is stubborn and doesn't want to admit defeat in his battle to maintain some sort of independence. But that's not possible anymore and so I repeat it to him that he needs help to avoid any further accidents. He nods and accepts that from now he will have to call for help rather than struggle on his own.

Petal appears to remain asleep during our chat but when I call out and ask her if she is alright, a faint but perky voice pipes up:

'Yes, thank-you.'

This is all I need to know – she is listening. But it's also understood that she doesn't need or necessarily want to join in any meaningful conversation. She is tired all the time now and sleeps for most of the day. In the afternoon, she is taken away to nap in her bed rather than in her chair beside Pop so that she won't suffer from sores on her skin from sitting in the same position all day. Pop says that she is 'remarkable' because she is so old and yet, as he points out, she keeps coming back from her injuries and ailments to face another day. And it's true: Petal is a tough cookie and is staying alive against the odds. But it's not much of a life for her any more – it's just an existence, and one that is seeing a virtual breakdown of her relationship with her husband. They are together for most of the day but they do not communicate very much. Pop will reach out and try and hold her hand but they don't talk – Petal is either asleep or Pop will be unable to hear what she says because his hearing aid is seldom able to pick up the sound of her voice.

Pop begins to cry saying, 'She doesn't talk to me anymore,' and I can only try to reassure him that at least they have had some great times together and that they have said all that needed to be said.

Pop talks to me about the accident when Petal had earlier fallen over. He says that after she fell the care workers had taken her to her room where she was seen by a doctor. Pop wanted to make sure she was alright so he had left his own room and had shuffled off down the corridor to check up on her. As he came to Petal's room he could see her being put to bed. He is breaking down into tears as he explains that he 'caught sight of the skeleton'.

A 'skeleton': This is how he is moved to describe the appearance of his wife as she was undressed by the care staff. I am shocked to hear these words and look over to see if Petal has heard and whether she has taken offence but her eyes remain closed and there is no reaction.

How can I imagine what that must be like for Pop – to see the devastating impact of age on his partner – the young, vibrant woman who became the love of his life, but who is now reduced to a 'skeleton?'

Old Photos

I am busy clearing up Dad's office for him and I take some time out, sit down at his chair and look up to the walls. There are some old framed photos hung up of Dad in the school football team and one of him in his Cambridge University tennis team. The colours have turned to sepia but my father looks fit and healthy. He is young, handsome and vibrant - a whole life ahead of him. In a couple of years from then, he will meet my Mum at his local tennis club and they will fall in love and marry. They will go skiing on their honeymoon and later make their home in Shropshire.

Time will be kind to them but they are good people and they have deserved all the luck they have had in life.

I look on the desktop and I notice a sheet of paper with Dad's handwriting on it. It is entitled *'Last Six Months.'* And then to the right of that heading is another one - it says *'Goals Before'* but that has been crossed out several times. The list includes sorting out all his finances and getting important family photographs in order.

Had Dad come up here before going into hospital knowing that he was nearing the end of his life?

Was *'Goals Before'* an incomplete *'Goals Before I Die'*?

Instinct tells me it was.

Dad, I have to conclude, must have suspected how seriously ill he was even before his diagnosis, and I feel desperately sorry for him once again. I hate the fact that he must have sat up here planning what he needed to do as he realised his future could soon be snatched away from him. I wonder how it must have felt for him to think that he perhaps had just months to live and now that time has been shortened even further.

After he has died Rebecca will send me the last pictures she had taken of Dad when I travelled down to Brighton to see them. Again, I read in Dad's face the story of a man who *knew* he was unwell. He looks like his smiles are slightly pained.

Something was wrong, and he knew it.

And how must he feel now, now that he has to leave behind his wife - the one and only real love of his life - and there is nothing he can do about it? What's it like for him to know that he will never get to see any of his children get married or have children? He has been denied the joys of being a grandfather. I know I'm being greedy and selfish but I so wish it could have been different for him, that he could have lived for just a few years more, to make it past seventy.

But we know there is no chance of that happening now.

I look at the wall and see an old, fading picture of Dad's parents. I think that perhaps one day I will be looking at an old picture of Dad and he will have died fifteen years ago and I will be in my fifties. I wonder if my Mum will still be alive then and how she will have coped after the death of my father.

There are two pictures of my Dad's grandparents – my great grandparents. I wonder if one day, a hundred years from now, someone - a young descendant of mine and my father's - will see a picture of me on a wall and give it a second thought. And should I even care? I know already that I do.

I remember going back to visit Shrewsbury school a few years ago where, like my own Dad, I had studied as a teenage boy. It was the first time I had been back in over fifteen years. I walked up the stairs of the boarding house where I had lived on and off for five years. Heading towards the dormitories, I stopped outside the laundry quarters. Here, I knew, were kept the old photographs of the pupils who once lived here. I wanted to see if I could spot myself in a picture from the now distant past.

I had stood at this spot when I was at school here. There I was all those years ago looking at the framed photos on the walls thinking about what had become of those boys now. The most recent pictures were in bright colour but as my eye-line passed down towards the older pictures I could see the yellowing of age setting into them. The last photographs in black and white were so faded that it was difficult to make out individual faces. These fourteen and fifteen year old boys that I could see before me would now be in their seventies; they will have lived their lives, some of them will be grandfathers, some of them will now be dead.

At that time, the pictures in which I appear are fresh and new but now the conveyor belt of time means that they are now in the middle section on the wall. My stomach drops as I stand there now and see that they too are now faded and are tinged with yellow. I can see myself and my house mates standing there smiling - young, fit, fresh and healthy.

I hate and detest time and decay and illness.

Old school pictures hung up on a wall are one thing but as I sit here now I think that today, in the modern Information Age of multi-media and mass communication, it's far harder to escape from wallowing in negative thoughts about your own physical decline. Every day on Facebook I can look at pictures of people I haven't seen for over twenty years and see how they have grown older, and know that I too am approaching middle-age. As I browse the pages of the Internet, I see people I once knew as children now living as grown-ups with kids of their own. Curly mops of hair have been replaced with receding hairlines; bright and ambitious eyes have been dulled with time.

I can indulge my nostalgia further by searching through footage on Youtube of former pop favourites. Memories will flood back of happy times, memories which fill me with sadness because they are now past.

Technology, perversely, is helping me – us - to live in the past, enabling us to turn inwards and drown in the aching melancholy of remembering lost moments, former love affairs, old friends, previously forgotten history.

As I sit there in Dad's office, I turn away from the computer in front of me and think back to when my grandparents died and remember Mum telling me how stunned my Dad appeared at his mother's funeral and I wonder how I am going to feel when Dad finally passes away. I am dreading it.

Dad's mother had taken her own life when she was well into her eighties. After the recent death of her best friend and a short battle with leukaemia, she'd decided enough was enough. She had run herself a bath and set up photographs of her husband, her son - my

Dad - and daughter, on the side of the tub. Then, after writing a final message to her children she passed a note beneath the front door of her apartment to alert her neighbour, and retreated back into her flat. She gathered up several tablets of morphine which she had kept hidden away for over twenty years, poured herself a glass of whisky, downed the pills, settled into a hot bath and there she died.

I wish Dad had the possibility of reaching the same age as his mother and to be able to end things at his own convenience, but it is not to be.

Part of me wants him to go quickly but I also want him to hang on and stay with us for as long as possible.

I wish we could all have a button that we could press.

All sorts of thoughts flood my mind. I've always been slightly obsessed with death and dying, but now, understandably I suppose, it's reached fever pitch. I torture myself with questions about basic human existence: what happens when we die? Why am I here? What is God's purpose? Does *He* even exist? That last one, I guess, is really *the* question that could help everything make sense. It's the question we all ask ourselves and it's the only one which really matters but which none of us can ever answer.

Blood and Bodies

As Dad lies in bed dying, I take a phone call. It is Janet - one of Mum and Dad's lifelong friends - she is aware that Hamesy is critically ill. She asks how long I think he has left to live. As soon as I had seen Dad back in hospital I thought he would be dead within two weeks. The doctors' diagnosis had been a slightly more optimistic figure and I pass on to Janet what Dad has been told – 'weeks not months.'

It will turn out that Dad will die on Janet's birthday.

Word is getting around of his illness and messages are pouring in. Every morning more cards arrive in the post, while throughout the day local folk hand-deliver their cards through the letterbox. The sound of cards dropping onto the floor in the hallway is the daily reminder that my Dad is valued and loved. But it's also the constant reminder that he is upstairs on what may turn out to be his deathbed.

There is something so incredibly surreal about all this. I feel like I have been transported back in time to Olde England. The town of Much Wenlock where my parents live is a small countryside village; it has a keen sense of history and tradition. I think of how this must have been the way it has always happened here over hundreds of years...local people pushing their handwritten notes of condolence through the door.

And now my Dad is becoming part of that history and we are stuck in the middle.

Mum and I sit at the kitchen table as another card is slipped through the letterbox and lands on the tiles set at the base of the front door. I go over and collect up the latest delivery. The cards are hard for us to read. They are affectionate and tender and they make Mum and I cry.

When I get up in the morning there are unopened letters addressed to Mum and she can't bring herself to open them all at once. It's too much for her to take. There's a backlog of cards that remain unopened. I open some of them up and place them alongside the hundreds of others that are now gathered on the dining room table and are spreading out across the surface of the kitchen.

I know that upstairs Dad can hear the sound of the cards being pushed through the letterbox. I think that he must know that people are rallying around and I hope he finds comfort in that and that it isn't upsetting for him. We have taken up a few of them for him to place beside his bed but we don't want to overwhelm him with too many.

For the moment I love the sound of a card landing on the tiles as another message is delivered. I love that sound because it is the sound of support and friendship for my Dad. But I will grow to hate that sound because in a short while this will be the sound of letters expressing sorrow at my father's passing and it will be the constant daily reminder that he is now dead.

But at least while he's still alive I can relish his presence; but I am also starting to worry about how his passing will affect me and the rest of the family - I realise how lucky I have been throughout my life, to have had two healthy, loving parents, to have been pretty much insulated from dying and death. I have never been in a car accident, never suffered any major injury or illness. Like everyone else, I have a degree of self-awareness, so I'd always been conscious that death is all around us...but I think - like a lot of people - I've always tried to keep it at bay, cut off and hidden. But you can't always deny its existence.

I remember once working on a TV documentary in America where I joined up with a team of crime scene cleaners for whom death was a real and vital part of life, not the abstract, distant menace that I'd quietly hoped it could always remain.

My first job teamed me up in San Fransisco with a guy called Doug – a veteran of hundreds of clean-up operations. We drove for a couple of hours until we reached a rather desolate looking motel complex just off one of the main highways into town.

Doug opened the door to room 111. Inside, the bed was dishevelled and had spots of blood and several smears of red on it. On the left, the door to the bathroom had been ripped off and lay on the floor. Huge pools of blood covered the walls and floor of the bathroom.

'Well, it's good that you're here,' said Doug with a friendly, resigned smile. 'A lot needs to be done.'

It was a gruesome sight. I leant my head into the bathroom. Fumes from days-old human remains reached into my nostrils.

'So do we know what happened here Doug, or not?'

'I know there was a stabbing. As far as the details go, I couldn't tell you.'

'And was this a murder?'

'Yes it was.'

For Doug this was just another regular job. He called his boss to let him know the details and described it as a four to five hour clean-up. The room would have to be completely gutted.

After kitting ourselves out in protective clothing, we set about our work. Together we lifted up the bathroom door from off the floor – it clung to the floor and then gave way with a horrible squelch to reveal a thick layer of deep red blood, the blood of a person who by now I had learnt had died here two days before. Despite wearing face-masks the stench was overpowering: the rich, metallic smell of congealed blood. I knelt down on the floor and began to wipe it clean. Blood was all over the bathroom – mainly on the floor but also splattered on the walls, and over the toilet and basin. In the shower, there were more patches of blood and hand prints leading up to the window.

The thick tissues I was using to wipe up blood off the floor had become quickly drenched. I was literally wiping up the last evidence of someone's existence and consigning it to the trash. Nausea overcame me as I felt myself imagining the scenes of frantic violence that had brought such a horrific scene to life. After a while I excused myself and headed off outside to try to get back to some normality.

I later discovered that the victim had been stabbed to death after being caught having an affair with someone else's wife. At the end of the day it was just one more grisly crime statistic of violent crime in America.

God, life can be so brutal.

We go to another clean-up operation later in the week – this time it's a female suicide victim in her teens. Another hotel room, but a different scenario: there is no sense of frenzy or violence, just one of deep sadness. There is a razor blade in the basin covered in thick, congealed blood. It is stuck to the cold white sink. I pull it off and place it in the bin. The bath tub is full of water and darkened blood. There are red smears on the toilet. Traces of blood line the walls, and I see a bloody hand print on the telephone by the side of the bed.

A half-eaten Macdonald's lies on a table top, the remnants of her last meal. A packet of cigarettes lies next to it. The ashtray shows a final, smoked cigarette. It all seems so trashy, so cheap, such a waste of a valuable life. I feel incredibly sorry for her. I wonder what had driven her to end her own life. I wonder who she had tried to phone and whether she had managed to speak to someone.

I wonder what her last thought had been.

I wonder too what my last thought will be.

We clean the room because the hotel has a business to run and will want to rent the room out again with as little delay as possible. From now on, when I stay in hotel rooms I will imagine whether it has previously played host to a suicide or a murder.

Cleaning up the physical remains of human life is still a step removed from seeing an actual body - a dead body - something I had never seen until that week in San Francisco. A visit to a morgue later on was to finally bring me face to face with a human corpse for the first time.

I remember as we open the doors to the freezer where the bodies are stored, I am hit with a blast of cold air. The unmistakable smell of death hangs heavy with a slight but tangible sense of decomposition. It has a nauseously rich twang.

In front of me are laid out somewhere in the region of twenty bodies. They have been put onto gurneys. White sheets have been placed over them but they fail to cover the bodies entirely. Some of the larger ones show faces, feet, arms and parts of torsos. There is one man, probably aged around sixty just a couple of yards ahead of me on the right. He is in a black body bag but he is a large man and they have not been able to fully zip him up. He is overweight and his stomach appears bloated. Folds of flesh press down on top of each other. His face is slightly discoloured – dark shades and bits of yellow. I can see several patches of dried blood on him. His right arm is fully visible showing his hand clenched into a claw-like fist.

Everything seems so incredibly still.

That hand will never move again.

Just across from me I can see the feet sticking out from another body. There is a case tag attached to his big toe and I can read that he died only yesterday. I imagine his family in despair. Opposite him lays a tiny figure completely wrapped up in white – it is a child, possibly even a baby or perhaps a still-born infant.

I wonder what has become of the mother.

There is a huge sense of sadness to see that someone so young has died, but I also find it oddly reassuring to be here and to see that these waxwork-like bodies seem to be mere cases, empty shells. I think of them as once living breathing human beings but now, to me, they are just pieces of cold flesh and dried blood. Something has gone from them - life obviously - but I can't stop myself from thinking that there has to be something else – a spirit - which divides the living from the dead.

And yet...it also seems so horribly final. These human bodies may just as well be dead animals, decomposing leaves; there is no division – they are just dead *things*.

We know, all of us, that this is where we will end up – as a dead body on a gurney in the freezer section of a morgue - but do we really allow that reality to truly sink in? Are we ignoring death, surrounding ourselves with life and the living in order to stave off an inevitable sense of dread and uncertainty? I know I do.

Back in England, I'm in the back of a cab in South London and see the signs to the local crematorium. We all see these signs - we have all, at one time or another, walked past a shop labelled Funeral Director. Hearses pass us on the street, a lone coffin in the back with flowers labelled 'DAD' or 'MOTHER'. We all sit on trains, look out of the window and see graveyards in the distance. But I'm not sure that we allow ourselves to fully register its impact. But why should we? After all - if you take God out of the equation - the prospect of death should, when you consider what it truly means, fill us with something approaching horror. I guess it's only natural to want to steer clear from such a terrifying reality, the thought of leaving loved ones behind, of never being able to satisfy long-held dreams.

The trouble for me – and, I assume, for others - is that I want to be prepared for death when it actually happens to me. And yet, like everyone else, I know I can never be fully prepared, because I don't know how or when or why it will happen to me.

Death and mortality is such a mess, such a losing battle. It's exhausting: I need a cigarette.

Open Coffin

A few days after Dad has died and his body taken away, Mum asks me if I want to go and visit him at the funeral parlour.

'Do you want to go and visit your Dad?' she asks.

It seems strange to still refer to him as 'Dad' because it sounds like he is still alive, sitting in a hospital bed somewhere. But it will not really be him, just his body. I want to go and see him though, because I want to have a different final memory of my Dad, I don't want my last memory of him to be witness to his final, struggling breaths – I want to see him at peace.

Mum and I arrange to visit him the next day.

We walk arm-in-arm to where Dad's body is being kept – we never normally do the walking arm-in-arm thing, but Dad's death seems, at least for the moment, to have brought us closer together, and it's nice for me to feel close to Mum. We turn the corner and walk up to the entrance to the funeral parlour. It is an old building right in the heart of town, just a few minutes' walk from where we live. It looks like the converted outbuildings of a barn and it is here, in a small family industry, where they build the coffins and store the bodies of the dead.

Mum and I are greeted in the courtyard by the local undertaker but we are soon left alone because Mum has already been here with my brother and she knows where to go. We walk into a low slung, old brick building, and there in the centre of a small room, is the open coffin which holds the body of my father.

I approach him. I don't know why but he somehow looks a little smaller than I remember - my father was six feet tall but the wooden coffin seems to be less than that. I look across at his face and am immediately struck with how handsome and dignified he looks. He looks really, really good. I can't remember if he had stubble when he died but I think he did and I suspect he has been shaved; his hair too has been combed. He looks quite thin but he looks better for it, and his skin colour is healthy looking. I don't know if they have put make-up on him but if they have they have done a really good job because it looks natural and understated.

I stand and look over to him; a huge sadness comes over me and I well up with tears.

Mum comes over to me and squeezes my hand.

'Are you alright?' she asks.

'Yes,' I tell her. 'I think he looks really good.'

Mum nods and moves away from me and looks down at Dad. I keep looking at my father's face. I think about whether to touch him or hold his hand or kiss him. My brother has placed a small card in my Dad's hand. I look at my Dad's fingers and see how gravity and rigor mortis have taken hold. They somehow appear heavy, sunken.

Suddenly, as my eyes move back up towards my father's face, I see his right cheek move in a spasm. It's like a miniature lightning bolt moving down from the cheek bone towards his mouth. What the hell is happening? I know it cannot really have moved *because he is dead*. I immediately flick my eyes over to Mum to see if she has registered anything unusual – *I swear, I just saw his face move* - but Mum has not flinched, she is still looking down at him and I know that I must be hallucinating in some way.

This is all very unusual.

Or is it?

Is this just part of how my brain is reacting to seeing my dead father in his coffin?

Is this trauma?

Is this normal? I don't think it is, but I'm not sure I know what normal is any more. And I'm not sure I even care. All I know is that I will not be sharing this information with my Mum – things have been crazy enough recently without me appearing to be completely losing the plot.

I try to relax because this is really important to me, to stand here and try to enjoy my final moments with my father: I want a happy last memory of him and this will be it. I am really glad that he looks so good, just like I hoped he would. I tell Mum that I think he looks really handsome and she agrees. He does look particularly striking. I move over to the other side of the coffin and look back down at him.

In my head I am saying a constant stream of goodbyes.

I stand for another few seconds and then I look over at Mum – it's time for us to leave.

My Friend, Nick

As I look ahead, I am dreading the thought of having to go to Dad's funeral. I think back to the last funeral I went to which was for a lovely friend and one of the stand-out characters at school.

My mate Nick was a huge lad – a great big bumbling fellow, tall, thick-set and built to last. He stood out a mile and had the personality to match, shunning authority and always being swift to entertain. He had been in the year below me at school and looked up to me as something of a guiding light.

One of the brightest, wittiest kids I had ever known, Nick had gone on to study Chinese after leaving school. Winning a place at university in London, Nick rented a room at my sister's flat in Battersea. This was great, because not only did it provide Rebecca with a fun flat-mate, but it also meant it was easy for us to stay in touch; whenever I visited London, Nick was there to make me laugh and provide the perfect company for a good night out on the town.

I knew that Nick, like me, was a bit of a tearaway; but what I didn't know was that drugs were swiftly becoming a major part of his life.

One day I met up with him. By now he had left my sister's flat but had returned to London after spending a year in Hong Kong as part of his studies. I had heard rumours that Nick had had an accidental overdose while abroad and so, sensing trouble and that something needed to be said, I asked him about it. Nick told me that he had scored some heroin and had gone to a public toilet to smoke it. That already sounded pretty sordid to me. Worse, he had then passed out, collapsed and banged his head on the toilet. Luckily, someone had found him and called the emergency services whereupon Nick was bundled into an ambulance. He had been declared dead en route but then, against the odds, they had revived him. Nick had eventually fully recovered and was able to walk out of hospital just a day later.

'Bloody hell Nick – that's insane!'

'I know – I got lucky.'

'Is that normal for you though – to take heroin?'

'Sure,' he replied. We never inject, but me and my mates enjoy a quick smoke of it if we're having a night out. It's so easy to get and doesn't really do anything – just makes you feel mellow.'

I had no idea.

'Fucking hell, Nick!'

'It's no big deal', he insisted. 'It's not like we take loads of it – just a quick puff here and there.'

'Were you just smoking it in Hong Kong or injecting?'

'I'd never inject it – I only smoked a little bit; it was just dodgy stuff, I think.'

I didn't like what I was hearing.

'Nick,' I said, 'you have to promise me – you can't do heroin again. This is your wake-up call – it's obvious – you're only smoking a little bit but it still affects you really badly – your body can't handle it so please don't do it, you really can't....you mustn't. Jesus.'

'I know, I know.'

I knew a no-drugs policy wasn't going to work with Nick but I knew had to say something to try and get him to change his ways.

'Listen, do me a favour – just do whatever drugs you want to do – smoke some weed, do a little coke – just do anything and everything you want to do but just don't do heroin. That stuff kills and you know that all too well now. OK? Please Nick. Look at me. You nearly fucking died!'

'Yeah; I know what you're saying.'

'Let's shake on it – do anything, just not heroin. Just promise me that.'

I offered him my hand and we shook.

'OK', he said. 'I won't.'

I left his flat later wondering if I'd said enough.

Just a few months later, I got a call from a mutual friend – 'I've got really bad news, Ash – Nick is dead. He died last night.'

I couldn't believe what I was hearing. But it was true: Nick had been in his flat watching television on a humdrum Tuesday evening and had retired upstairs to bed where he'd decided to take a quick smoke of heroin before going to sleep. He had passed out, been sick and had failed to wake up: Nick had apparently choked to death on his own vomit.

Had I said enough to dissuade him from taking heroin? Obviously not.

A few days later I get a call from Nick's sister, Naomi. She asks me to be a pall-bearer at Nick's funeral. That day arrives and I find myself in a car along with some of Nick's best friends following the hearse. They are trying to make light of it and crack off a few weak jokes. I stay silent and grim-faced. I can't believe that Nick is there in the car ahead of us, no longer alive, just a body in a box. He is so young; it seems so unfair, so unreal.

The cars stop outside a church and we get out. Because Nick is so heavy we are not expected to carry him into the church but instead we must lift him out of the hearse and place him on a trolley and wheel him in. We get in position and we lift the coffin. I can feel the huge weight of my dead friend inside and imagine him lying in there, grey, pallid, deathly, a physical reminder of a spent life. He's really, really heavy; a dead weight. It brings it home that there really is a person in there – my mate Nick.

We place him successfully on the trolley and then we push him up a small incline towards the entrance of the church. A nightmare scenario runs through my head – that Nick's coffin will slip off the trolley, the coffin will spill open and the stiffened body of my old school friend will roll out into the graveyard. We steady the coffin and push it up and into the church. I can't stop thinking of the person inside and how young and bright he is, a full-on funny, charming kid in his twenties.

And now that's it.

Is this really what fate had in store for Nick? Had this all been mapped out for him, to die in the full flush of youth, to make one, simple mistake that would end everything? Nick's early death had left his Mum bereft of her only son who she totally and utterly adored. How could this possibly make sense to his family, to his friends? It was such a tragedy and yet it's just one of thousands, hundreds of thousands.

I will vow to myself that day that I will never take drugs again. I hate drug dealers and I hate drugs because they have killed one of my mates and I swear that I want no part of them.

But in time, the passions that I feel that day will fade and I will take drugs again and I will enjoy them.

Which I suppose makes me a total, unadulterated asshole.

The service for Nick finishes and we take the coffin back outside. I catch a glimpse of my sister on the way out of the church and my face creases up with grief. Nick's own sister, Naomi joins my side, takes my hand and squeezes it and smiles at me. We walk outside together and then head off to the mortuary for a quick service for the family and a few close friends. The coffin lies before us, ominous. And then the curtains will open and - this is the same moment that will stay with me at my father's funeral – there is music and then there is movement and the coffin will slowly, slowly disappear from view. Then the curtains will close and that is the moment when you really do know that it is over, finished. As long as the coffin is still around, there is at least a physical presence, a reminder, the possibility that this is just a bad dream.

But now the music has finished and it is time to leave and you will never see this person that you loved, ever again.

DAY FOUR

Romance

I wake up and go downstairs to see how Dad is. He asks me very deliberately, for *'a Diet Coke with two cubes of ice.'* I have never seen him drink a Diet Coke in his entire life but he seems to be developing some odd cravings. Diet Coke is only stocked in the house for when I return home for my brief visits. I smile at him and repeat his order to check I've got it right: 'A Diet Coke?' And Dad repeats that he would like two cubes of ice. Two cubes, not three. I look down at him and smile briefly because I find all this strangely charming. When I return with his drink it seems to really hit the spot. He stops me as I move to depart and thanks me for helping Mum and for looking after him. After all he's done for me it seems ludicrous that he should feel the need to thank me simply for lending a helping hand.

'Dad,' I reply. 'You really don't have to say thank-you. It's fine.'

He then asks me if I am sleeping alright. On top of a troublesome recent period at work where sleep had been scarce, I now haven't slept for more than maybe two hours a night since I got back home, but I lie and tell him I had a really good night's sleep. I don't want him worrying about me: I just want him thinking everything is alright and that we are coping well.

'And how's your Mum?'

'Well,' I begin, 'I think she's alright, but you know, it's obviously difficult but I think she's coping pretty well.'

Dad looks across at me. He's lying on his side. He has a sick bowl by his stomach and a small cloth in his hand to wipe his mouth.

'How are you feeling about things, Dad?' I ask.

'Well,' he replies, 'I suppose one positive thing is that this has come at a time when your Mum is still young enough to find someone else after I have gone.'

Dad is being his usual sensitive, thoughtful and rational self but it must surely pain him to have to think that this could be the case: that Mum could end up being with a new partner some time ahead in the future, after he has gone. But he doesn't sound or look upset; he just says it as though it's the most normal thing in the world, a fact of life; a fact of death.

I nod but don't say anything. I don't want to give this any thought for now, but I guess my first reaction is to hope that he is right: that Mum can eventually move on after this and find happiness with someone else. Dad looks away from me and up towards the ceiling, alone with his thoughts. Again I wonder how the realisation that my Mum - the one, true love of his life - could end up in a relationship with another man in his absence is making him feel. He does seem to have selflessly accepted it as a possibility. I suspect he is perhaps thinking back to his own Mother who, after the death of her husband, had a brief but enjoyable relationship with someone else when she was well into her seventies.

I don't mention this to Mum – it's hardly appropriate right now - but I do finally talk to her about the trouble I am having trying to sleep at night. I don't tell her the whole story though, and make it sound like I'm catching at least several hours a night (I wish). I ask her how she is doing, because like me, she looks really tired. She answers that she is doing OK and managing to sleep a little. I think we may both be lying to each other in order to protect one another. At the moment, Dad interrupts her during the night with the two-way phone every three or four hours for medication. I don't offer to take over the job of nursing him because I know she wants to do that and to be responsible for how he feels. It must be shattering for her but I am proud of her. She is fighting this in such a lovely way, keeping everything ticking along, moving forward towards the inevitable.

There is a very real romance about all this – this is the final chapter of Mum and Dad's own love story. It's a sad ending, but it's one of which I think they can both be really proud.

Of course, it's also the final chapter of me and my father's relationship, and one that I want to end with me having finally told him that I love him. We'd gone 37 years without it being said, but now, with my emotions raw, that sentence has floated to the surface. There was no urgency before, but now there is. Besides, I think he'll like to hear it and I think it will be good for him to say it back. As time slips away, I hate the thought that I will fail to tell him how much he meant to me; I need to do this, and soon.

Mum and I sit and talk quietly about Dad. He is just a stone's throw away upstairs and we both feel his presence and when we break down crying we try to keep our sobs muffled so he doesn't hear us and become upset. It is strange how we are crying – we will be in the middle of a conversation and then mid-sentence one of us will crease up and tears will fall. And then seconds later we will be alright and manage to continue talking. Seeing her cry makes me break down with sadness, but soon we will recover and be alright again and our conversation will carry on. There is no wailing, no howling in anger, just a steady but unpredictable release of grief, a tap which turns on and off.

Time will mean these tearful moments will become more infrequent, but no less painful.

When I am visiting Mum over a year after my father has died we sit and chat and I will be reminded about Dad's last moments. We are talking about my granddad Pop, because he is seriously ill at the moment and I have returned home to Shropshire after a phone call from Mum telling me he had been taken by ambulance into hospital after collapsing at the care home. She is explicit about it, warning me that her own father could now be on his last legs. It's no surprise: we have all been expecting this for some time.

Pop is in Telford hospital. Mum and I will visit him later on.

As I sit with Mum, I remind myself of when Pop told me of having fought in the Second World War. I assume, because of the trauma of conflict, Pop had always been reluctant to talk about the war, but as he grew much older he began to open up a little, and one of his stories had always stuck with me. Once, Pop and another soldier were in a cemetery in Italy trying to defend themselves from some attacking German infantry. They were positioned just a couple of yards from each other behind single gravestones in a bid to stay sheltered from flying bullets and shrapnel. While taking pot shots at the enemy, a grenade flew over and landed in between them, just a few feet away. Pop recalled seeing the grenade and looking over at his colleague to say a last goodbye: both men believed they were just seconds from death. And then, the grenade failed to detonate – one tiny piece of malfunctioning metal: such are the tiny margins that divide life and death.

Months later, he and some fellow soldiers had fought and taken over a small farm-holding in the Italian countryside. As my grandfather stood at the door after battle to survey their position, he heard the crack of a rifle in the distance and was suddenly hit in the shoulder. The bullet passed straight through his back missing his vital organs by a matter of centimetres – he survived and went on to make a full recovery.

My grandfather had been incredibly lucky on two separate occasions and I was left wondering how life would have turned out if that grenade had gone off, or if that bullet had been an inch or two closer to his heart. Surely then, my Mum's life would have taken a completely different course - would she have ever met my Dad? Would I have even been born? - Probably not.

And then of course I think of my Dad and wonder where that first cancer cell had come from? And why did it have to be terminal and not benign? And then my thoughts spin out even further and I'm revisited by the acute sensation of how amazingly fragile life can be – why does one random car crash lead to death and destruction and another leave its victims uninjured? Does fate play a factor or is luck the only thing that keeps us from an early death? All I know is that I am bad at goodbyes and when my turn arrives I want to take a sudden hit. I don't want to suffer; I don't want to know when death is *happening* to me. And now, I wonder, as my granddad lies desperately ill in hospital, if death is there now, waiting for him.

Mum and I get up and make the car journey to go and see him. We walk into Pop's ward at Telford hospital but stop briefly to talk to two of the nurses who have just been attending to him. I look over at my grandfather: lying there in bed he looks so ill, so damn old. I suddenly have a horrible feeling that just yards away stands the abstract figure of Death looking over my granddad, ready to take him. The walls are closing in and I'm reminded immediately of back when my own Dad was lying in bed...waiting. Here with Pop, I sense somehow that the figure of Death is standing to my left, looking – like me – towards my grandfather – anticipating his final moments. I want to stride over to this presence and beat the living daylights out of him and tell him where to shove his scythe.

I don't do that though because I would be swinging punches at mid-air. It would look bloody weird. I'd also be shouting obscenities at....nothing.

I hold my ground and glance back over at Pop and I worry that he doesn't appear to be breathing. *He's not dead already is he?* I hate to think it but I can't stop myself: he looks like a corpse. I know I'm being a bit irrational and alarmist though - he surely couldn't be dead – the nurses were with him just moments ago. But his mouth is hanging slightly open; his body is completely still and slightly discoloured. I glance back to the nurses who are still chatting to Mum. I'm not listening any more. I hear a vague stream of words, I see a smile or two, but nothing is making much sense to me. I want to go over and see Pop, make sure he is OK. I want to do that right now. Mum then turns towards me and we finally walk over to him.

Pop's eyes are closed. Mum looks down at him and she puts her hand on his head.

'Hello Pop,' she says with unbelievable tenderness.

Pop opens his eyes and they brighten as he sees her, and then he catches sight of me standing next to his daughter and I can see the flicker of recognition and an instant of delight before his eyes close again. It's a brief but heart-warming moment which I will never forget. I place my hand on his shoulder and give him a tiny squeeze. He struggles to say a little 'hello' but he is so exhausted and cannot say anything.

'You've been through the mill, haven't you Pop?' I say out loud to him with what I hope is a hint of encouragement that he can get better.

Pop looks at me and tries to smile but I can see in his eyes that he hasn't grasped what I have just said to him.

'He hasn't got his hearing aid in, Darling,' my Mum says. 'He can't hear a word you're saying.'

Blimey, sometimes I feel like such a muppet.

Pop opens his eyes one more time for just a couple of seconds and I get a flash of understanding, a sense that he is hugely disappointed with himself that he is unable to hear or talk to us. I think he feels inadequate, stripped of dignity, done in; I think he feels like he's had enough; he is finished.

I am a bit shocked at how old and run-down he looks: he does not have his false teeth in and because of that his face appears a little collapsed; it helps to age him considerably. His feet twitch a little but apart from that there is nothing, just the faint sound of him breathing, the occasional moan. He has scarcely eaten for days and looks desperately thin. Mum moves her hand across his hair to comfort him.

'Alright,' she says. 'It's alright.'

She continues stroking his hair to help her father settle back to sleep. Again, I have flashbacks to Mum lying next to my Dad as he lay dying and she is stroking his head.

'Alright,' she repeats, soothing her father.

Pop looks fairly peaceful but he has no energy to communicate and it's obvious to both of us that he will die soon. I look around the ward and see a man around my age with what looks like a dislocated knee or a broken leg in the bed opposite. It seems odd that someone like that is in the same ward as my granddad, someone who will walk out of here in a couple of days and carry on with his life. But this is *it* for my granddad and I think everyone knows that, including Pop himself.

After a minute or two we leave. Mum kisses Pop's forehead and I begin to turn away because I want Mum to be able to say her goodbye away from me and if I stay any longer I think I am going to get upset and start crying. I am just a few yards away from his bed when Mum joins me and I consider whether to turn back and look towards Pop again but I decide not to because I don't want to drag the moment out. I also have the sense that if I look back round, then that moment will be the last time I will ever see my granddad. But I have already had that moment and do not turn back.

Mum and I get back home and sit down and talk about Pop and whether we think he will survive and how long we expect him to live.

'He won't recover from this,' Mum says.

'I know,' I reply.

And then I think back to that unsettling presence that I felt in the hospital, that ominous feeling that Death was in the room with us. Yet again I am reminded of when Dad was upstairs in bed and having the same feeling back then - that Death was standing by the door waiting to claim his latest victim.

'I just know Pop won't survive...'

I stop talking because my face is starting to collapse in grief. For a moment, Pop is forgotten and instead I am left again with a searing sense of the loss of my own father. I can't believe that more than a year after his death it is still so intense a feeling. I am shocked, upset and overwhelmed by my own propensity to lapse back to *exactly* how I felt in the first wave of grief for my father.

Time has not blunted the pain in any way whatsoever.

Mum sees my distress. 'Oh, Darling,' she says.

She gets up from her chair and walks over to sit next to me on the sofa.

'What are you thinking?' She asks. 'That we've been here before?'

I can't really reply and don't especially want to tell her that, even if she knows it herself, I can see Death looming over her own father just as it had once been there for mine. Mum sits with me for a while and we go back to talking about how, for Pop, this is probably all for the best: he is very old, he has been increasingly unhappy, there is little or no value left in his life. But I am still really thinking about Dad and how I wish that he was still there with us and how he could have comforted Mum so much better than I can at the moment.

I wonder if, in Dad's absence, I am really, truly doing enough to help my Mum – although I speak to her every week, this is the first time I have been home for several months. When I promised Dad that I would look after her, have I followed that through with real commitment? Have I repaid his faith in me or have I let him down? I doubt I will ever be able to do enough, but I do think Mum is doing OK; trouble is, now that Pop appears to be at death's door there will be added pressure to try and help out. But Mum is always trying to encourage me to stay in London and I know why – she knows that I too have a life to lead and the last thing she wants is for me to start tearing myself up about how she is feeling.

I ask Mum if Petal has been told about where Pop has disappeared to. Barring his absence during the war, Petal and Pop have been together virtually every day for more than seventy years. Despite the fact that he has been gone from the home for nearly a week - and that they have spent every day there together in the same room - Mum tells me that Petal has not asked about him once. I find it difficult to get my head around this. To be so long together and for him to disappear must have triggered off something, surely? Part of me thinks that Petal might know that something is up, and that she is aware that we are trying to shield her from any distress. But Petal herself is more and more absent from her own body.

The only surprise of recent events is that it is looking increasingly likely that Petal will outlive her husband – we always thought it would be the other way round.

Everything is so unpredictable.

I wonder how Petal will react if – when - Pop dies. It won't be long.

Sleep

Later on today, my father's sister Sue is coming to visit.

Mum and I have been chatting about this and my mother is fretting slightly that this may be a traumatic and distressing experience for them both. I'm also a bit concerned: the day before I had been talking to Dad and he flagged up how important it was for me to nurture my relationships with my brother and sister.

'Stay close to them Ashley,' he said. *'One day they are going to be the only people who you will have known your whole life.'*

For Dad, family was everything. And now his sister, his only sibling, was coming to say her goodbye.

A couple of days previously I had spoken to Sue on the phone to break the news about Dad; I knew that Sue's husband was also critically ill in hospital, and now I had to tell her that her brother was dying of cancer. I heard the sound of sobbing on the end of the line and we then made arrangements for her to visit. That day had now arrived.

Sue drove up with her daughter Fiona – my Dad's goddaughter - and after a while, she headed upstairs to see her brother. Mum and I held our breath, but it turned out we didn't really need to. When I later go and see Dad, I ask him if he's alright and he replies '*sure*', as though it didn't really register with him that my question was loaded with the unsaid *'Are you OK because you may have just seen your sister for the last time?'*

When I probe him a little and ask him how his conversation with Sue went, he says they had a really nice chat but he is completely matter-of-fact about it. I can't help thinking that of all the people involved in this tragedy, Dad is handling it better than anyone else. I suppose he is at the point where there is nothing he can do about it and that helplessness is, in a strange way, giving him a sense of serenity, that this is how it has to happen and that's the way it will be. His weakness, his helplessness, is actually giving him strength. When your destiny is no longer in your own hands, then I guess there's no more peaceful place, and that, I assume, is the place where my Dad now finds himself.

Fiona also goes to visit him and, several years down the line, she will write to me to tell me how lucky she felt to be able to say goodbye, how it had felt so precious, and how she had shared one of the most intimate moments of her life with him, knowing it would be the last time she would ever see him.

I wonder what was said in these moments.

When Fiona joins us downstairs after seeing my Dad, I wonder if she had found the strength that had so far been lacking in me to tell my Dad that she loved him. It would be so nice for him to hear that from me as well as from others, and I'm desperately frustrated that I still haven't had the guts to say it.

Later on, the local Doctor comes round to the house to check up on Hamesy. I greet him with a smile at the door but see a very dour expression looking back at me. To try to brighten his mood, I deliver my own take on the Livingstone legend and so greet him with a droll *'Dr Matthews, I presume.'* Unsurprisingly, given the circumstances, my lame attempt at humour is lost on him. I feel a bit stupid for trying to make light of a grave situation.

Chastened, I usher him upstairs to talk with Dad and leave them alone. Afterwards, he comes downstairs and Mum speaks to him. The Doctor tells Mum that he's never arrived at a situation like the one my father's in to find that he is leaving the house feeling better, more peaceful than when he arrived. Usually when dealing with people facing death head-on he would retreat feeling disturbed, restless. Somehow, Dad has reassured him that he's fine about it, that it's alright.

Dad, it would appear, is far more relaxed than the rest of us.

Shortly before leaving, the Doctor turns to my Mum and says,

'And I shall no doubt be seeing you coming by the clinic in a few weeks' time.'

What does he mean by that? I'm not sure I like what I have just heard and feel protective towards my mother. How do I interpret that? Does he think she is going to be unable to cope, that she will become dragged into a pit of depression when faced with the death of her husband? Maybe my Mum will end up going stir-crazy with despair but I don't want that and I don't want the possibility of it being mentioned. I worry that he may just dish her out some pills to keep the pain, the grief, at bay.

Or maybe I'm being over-protective towards my mother and misreading an entirely innocent comment.

Whatever, my concerns are dismissed a day later, when I ask Mum to get some sleeping pills from him so I can finally get some rest at night. The same Doctor refuses to let her have any, citing their addictive qualities. I'm annoyed that I can't get something to help me sleep but at the same time, part of me is glad that Mum's GP is no walkover. Back in London I'm used to being able to get what I want when I want, and in the past, mainly due to work pressures, that has included sleeping pills. But life is different up here. This is old-style, small town rural England, where people look out for each other and where the undertaker will turn out to be the odd-job man who did some handy-work for Dad in the months before he first became ill.

When Mum and I head off during the day for the short walk to the shops we are asked about Dad by some of the people who live there. It seems like everyone in the village knows that he is terminally ill and that gives us a good feeling – that we are not alone in this, that support is out there. Mum, I am happy to see, has a strong network of friends.

When I go into the chemist to get some Nightol I am asked if I have taken it before. I am astonished that they would even bother to ask me the question and I am angered by it because I haven't slept properly for days and I need to sleep, I am desperate for it; I really, really need to sleep. But at the same time, I feel like I am being looked after.

Six months later, following the death of my father, I am alone in my flat in London and I don't have the same feeling that I did back home with Mum – that I am valued and cared for. I have to look after myself and I'm learning fast that I'm not very good at that.

For starters, my sleep patterns are still all over the shop: I go to bed at around 2am but I wake up – without fail - an hour or two later. This is happening every single night and it is doing my head in. It's relentless. My brain is in overdrive as if I am wide awake yet I feel utterly ruined. I am officially a train wreck.

Physically I am totally shattered, yet I am completely alert with a thousand and one thoughts swirling around in my head. My eyes are swollen and bloodshot. I traipse along to the bathroom and look at myself in the mirror: Talk about death warmed up - I look absolutely bloody dreadful. My skin is pale, colourless; my eyes make me look like a drug addict: the eyelids are purple and have turned into hoods so that I have an almost permanent squint. Small blood vessels are bursting on my nose and cheeks. I look like total crap.

I walk over to my front room and chain-smoke my way through a pile of cigarettes while watching any old nonsense that happens to be on telly at four in the morning. I know that the cigarettes will act as a stimulant but I really don't care - my aim is to smoke myself into feeling so ill and rundown that I will have to collapse into bed and hopefully catch a few more hours sleep.

My living standards have reached new lows - I have given up even bothering to use ashtrays – there are cups and glasses overflowing with cigarette butts mixed in with the residue of stale coffee, wine, and old tea bags. Some of my plates have ciggies stubbed out in leftover food which is now days old and counting. Empty fag packets are strewn on the floor. More unwashed plates and cups are left discarded in the kitchen. Piles of laundry are waiting to be washed. My flat is beginning to look like a squat.

I need to start caring a bit more but all I care about right now is sleeping and feeling normal again. Nothing else matters to me. I would pay serious money right now for just 4 or 5 hours straight sleep. Sleep used to be my best friend. Now it's my worst enemy.

By eight or nine in the morning I am full up on nicotine and tar and feel rough as fuck. I neck a glass of red wine and wince as it burns the back of my throat. The plonk is cheap swill and I hope it adds to the pain of feeling so damn rough that I will have to sleep it off. The plan works to some degree as my lungs are starting to heave when I move about. I blow my nose and I see the tissue is splattered with blood. My mouth tastes rancid. I feel so fucking crap it's untrue. I go to bed and lie there desperate for sleep. I put in some wax earplugs and wear an eye-mask to shut myself off. Eventually, after twisting and turning like a maniac as I scratch around for a dose of shut-eye, I fall into a welcome snooze. Thank God - I have finally dozed off.

A couple of hours later I wake up and it's now mid-afternoon. I'm so grateful to be a bit rested but it's all so maddening: just when life has hit me with the realisation that time is short and vital, I am spending most of it trying to sleep. I am wasting endless hours, days – weeks - of my short life.

By the fifth or sixth week of identical non-sleep patterns I am starting to really freak out. I wake up in the usual 3-4am slot and feel levels of frustration that are through the roof. My first action when I wake and see the time is to smash my fist violently down on top of my duvet. Then I grab my pillow and scream into it 'Fuck! Fuck! FUCK!'

Then, no words, I just scream.

The pillow muffles my shouting so that I don't wake my neighbours living above me.

I calm myself down with another cigarette or four and decide to try and stay awake for the rest of the day. I hope that by doing this I will feel sufficiently exhausted that when I go to bed later that night I will be bound to crash out and have a good night's sleep. I wend my way through the day in a zombie-like state and eventually night arrives and I stagger into bed. I read for a while to take myself through till past midnight and then I close my eyes and drift off.

When I wake up, I feel fully alive and I think that I have broken the mould - it must now be morning. I do a mental guess and hazard that it may be around 7 or 8 o'clock. It had bloody well better be. Please, *please* let me have had a decent night's kip; it's not too much to ask for is it? I sit up and look at the time on my bedside clock. Oh strike a frigging light! It's 1.20 am. Oh Jesus Fucking Christ *No!* I have had just over an hour's sleep.

I feel doomed, hopeless.

I feel like giving up.

I am losing the plot.

I feel like if someone was to walk into my flat right now with a loaded gun I would happily grab it, put it against my head and pull the trigger. I am in a bad, bad place.

I gently lie back down, turn over on my side and then after a few minutes I heave myself out from under my duvet. I sit on the side of the bed and stay there for a few seconds. I feel so incredibly angry with myself. I grab my pillow and scream into it again. Then I scream again, louder this time, a proper Neanderthal blast right from the pit of my stomach, my face buried in the pillow. I want to cry and try and force myself to let go, to let it all out, to cry and give vent to my frustration. I want to make myself feel better. A couple of tears drop but they feel forced and unnatural and this makes me feel even more pissed off.

I feel close to breaking down but I'm on the verge, not quite there – I'm in no-man's land, stuck in some kind of limbo. Rather than just tinker around the precipice I feel myself actually wanting to sink further, to go down into a really low place, to suffer a proper mental breakdown. In some perverted way, I actually want to completely crack up, just so that I can begin to make some kind of proper recovery.

I really feel like I can't take this anymore; I want to see a Doctor.

That's what I need to do – I have to see a Doctor, I have to get some sleeping pills and knock this on the head.

I do the usual time-wasting / heart-attack / terminal cancer-inducing routine, doze off for an hour or two and then pull on some clothes and head off down to my local surgery. I feel like such a loser and look like an absolute waster. I am desperately hoping that I don't see any locals who I might know or who may recognise me. I have shades on to hide the worst of it. Eventually my name is called and I remove the sunglasses and my head kicks back a little as the daylight hits me. I make my way through to see my GP and sit down. He asks me what the problem is and I give him a blow-by-blow account of my recent sleep issues.

After I am finished he asks if I am doing any exercise.

'No. I haven't done anything for a while. I feel like I need to.'

'Yes, that might help. What about work? Are you working at the moment?'

'On and off,' I reply.

'Are you still drinking?'

'Yes. But less than I was a few years ago.'

'And how's everything things else going?'

'Well...' – and as I speak I feel my face begin to contort - '...not great...my Dad died a few months ago...'

Suddenly, without any further preamble, I crack up and begin to cry. Having tried not to think too much about my father, I am right back in full-on upset mode. Tears are pouring down my face and dropping off my chin onto my clothes. I haven't cried like this in months and I can't quite believe I still feel so fervently raw at the mere mention of my Dad. I thought I was getting over it, getting better, pushing my Dad to the back of my mind, but It's like someone has just pricked me and the bubble has burst. I am taken aback and shocked at myself. This wasn't meant to happen.

'Sorry,' I say as I try to recover myself.

He reassures me and I welcome the sound of his voice.

'That's OK, it's perfectly normal.'

'Yeah; I've just found it really upsetting.'

'Of course,' he says.

My Doctor is being so sweet and kind to me and it's really comforting to hear him sympathise. I get myself back together and he asks me if I would like to see a grief counsellor and I say I will think about it but I don't want to commit to anything yet. I know my Mum has been seeing someone and she has mentioned to me that Adam, my brother, was planning on doing the same after suffering from a series of nightmares. I have told my Mum nothing about how bad things are for me right now – she has enough to worry about without me in the mix.

When I tell the Doctor that I don't feel that seeing a counsellor is something I necessarily want to do, he says that's fine and that he will give me a two week prescription for some sleeping pills. I immediately feel like cracking open a bottle of champagne and celebrating the sense of relief that I feel right now. I also feel purged from having cried properly for the first time in what seems like ages. After thanking him, I leave and head off to my local chemist where I hand my prescription over the counter as if it was a winning lottery ticket.

As soon as I get home I neck a tablet and get my first full stretch of sleep for months. It's beautiful. I feel joyful. I have slept from 5 in the afternoon until 4 in the morning. I don't care that for the moment I am again out of sync with the outside world; I am simply delighted to have slept for more than the usual two hours. Relief pours over me, and afterwards I run myself a bath and the water settles around me in waves of comfort. I am so happy to be back up and running. Instantly, I feel like a normal, functioning human being again. I am back in the land of the living and it feels so damn good.

The whole of the next week is bliss: the pills are knocking me out at night and I don't feel drowsy during the day. It's perfect: this is hopefully shifting me back into a normal pattern of sleep. My mood has completely changed from feeling desperate to one of real happiness.

The pills though, are becoming fewer. What happens when they run out? But no, I reassure myself that I am now sleeping at normal times and getting a full night's sleep – the habit should take hold. It had bloody better.

Two weeks in and I am out of pills. I go to bed and start to feel the pressure. What if I can't sleep again? I don't think I could handle that. I miss the bitter taste of the tablet in my mouth, the taste of The Promised Land of Nod. I push my fears away, flick off the light switch and turn over to sleep.

Then I awake. I'm fully alert.

I peek over at the clock.

It's 1am.

I have slept for one hour.

Dread fills me.

I try to sleep again. I lie there for hours but it's useless: nothing doing. I get out of bed, heavy with disappointment, and sit down in front of the telly where I stay for hours smoking cigarettes and drinking tea, my eyes glazed and frozen towards the screen.

I fret and I worry. Why is this happening? Why can't I sleep?

I am so gutted: I'm right fucking-shit-bastard back to where I started. I am a lost cause.

A month or two passes and it's the same old, same old. I am holding out though: I'm determined not to go back to see my GP. I don't want to get dependent on pills in order to sleep; I want to get some natural rest like everyone else. It's no use though: I feel dysfunctional.

I am getting really worried about my state of mind – not only can I scarcely sleep, but when I do eventually get some kip, I am having really bad nightmares about my parents. In one of them we are sitting as a family around the kitchen table having supper. My Mum has tears running down her cheeks and I don't understand why. Absolute and pure sadness is in the air. I turn and look at my Dad who is sitting beside me and he is completely grey and his clothes are worn through and I can see his body beneath all patchy and decaying. He looks extremely ill. Bits of rotting flesh are dripping off him like wax. He has a blank stare and looks sorrowful and upset. My brother and sister are there but no-one speaks. We are a silent, grieving family and my father is dead but still among us.

When I wake up I will be scared to go back to sleep even though it's the thing that right now I want and need most in the world.

My body is also completely shot – I feel heavy and docile. I'm rattling through cigarettes like there's no tomorrow – and at the rate I'm going there probably won't be. My addiction is so predictable that as soon as I push open the door to my local cornershop, the newsagent turns his back to the cigarette counter as soon as I enter to pass me a packet of Marlboro Lights without a word being spoken.

I am also eating way too much trashy food. I am eating to pass the time. I am trying to fill myself up, trying to find satisfaction somewhere. I am beginning to finally understand what they mean by 'comfort eating.' I can't remember the last time I ate any fruit or fresh vegetables – I'm eating complete junk. I am putting on weight and trying to disguise my fast-developing pot-belly by wearing loose jumpers and overcoats.

I have also bought some foundation to wear as light make-up in case I run into someone I know during the day: I'm hoping this takes the edge off the bags under my eyes and the redness of my skin. I am looking so damn awful and I don't want to have to explain to anyone that it's because I can't seem to catch a decent night's sleep to save my life.

I can't go on like this. I decide to give up and go back to the doctor's surgery. I need to sleep and I need help. It's a different doctor this time but I tell her the story and she reads my file history. She tells me about the problems of using sleeping pills and explains that users tend to have to continually up their dosage for it to have the same effect. She warns me that, should this happen to me, I could run the risk of addiction and end up in a zombie-like state some years down the line. I think to myself that I'm already in a zombie-like state from lack of sleep so what's the bloody difference? She's right though and we agree to give me ten days' supply of pills and that I should return if things don't improve.

Then she opens up a folder and hands me a questionnaire which she explains is designed to pinpoint depression in patients. I'm guessing she wants me to do this because insomnia is one of the symptoms of depression so I agree to fill it in which I do quickly, instinctively and truthfully.

I hand it back and she tots up my score.

On the depression front, she explains, I rate as having a 'very high score.'

Great: now I'm an insomniac *and* depressed.

DAY FIVE

Adam

Dad is using most of the little time and energy he has left by getting his affairs in order. There are bits and pieces of a small business he ran that need to be sorted out. They don't have any major financial implications but he wants to tidy everything up before he goes.

Mum and I talk about how he's being so obsessive about clearing the business up and we laugh a bit about it because it seems slightly ridiculous. I tell Mum I'm a bit surprised that at a time like this Dad isn't imparting worldly words of wisdom to me; he isn't even giving me the usual pep talks. There are no father / son conversations along the lines of, 'now when you get married and have children, son…'

Not a jot.

For the moment, 'The Vicar' is nowhere to be seen.

I'm almost put out!

Come on Dad – where's the Final Sermon?!

But there is none of that – instead, he's having me clear up some old stock that he has left in the office. Mum and I can't help but smile: this isn't quite what we expected.

What we realise is that, while he's alive, he wants to get his business all sorted out now to save us the trouble later - and so we do just that. It's his time not ours, and if that's what he wants to do then that's what will be done.

I wonder if I found myself in his position what I would be doing, what I would want to say to my family. I soon come to appreciate that for Dad and I, there's not a huge amount that really needs to be said. Before he fell ill, we would speak about what everyone talks about – things you've been up to, what you're planning for the future. Topics of conversation have always been fairly typical – football, career, politics. It's mainly small talk, the occasional deeper discussion, a rare argument. But now, none of those things matter and you find there's not much left to say.

Not much to say? There's still the unsaid 'I love you Dad.'

Aside from saying these words, what I crave most is to be in Dad's presence. That doesn't mean I even have to be in the bedroom with him, it's enough to just know he is in the house with me, alive, breathing, content. Being with Dad is - and always has been - time well spent.

I ask Dad if he would like a radio or television in the bedroom to help keep him company and he looks at me as if I have gone slightly crazy. I understand in an instant how ridiculous this suggestion must have sounded to him. He doesn't want to have distractions; he wants to be alone with his thoughts and prepare for what's ahead.

I have another sleepless night and go downstairs in the early hours to see if Dad is awake. I walk softly into his room. There's a small light on in the corner of the room. He's facing away from me but senses that I'm there or perhaps he has heard me coming down the stairs. He can't turn around because that will make him uncomfortable so he lifts an arm off the bed to let me know that he is awake and that I can come in and talk to him, that I'm not disturbing him.

'Hi Dad, are you alright?'

'Yes. I've had to wake your Mum up once or twice tonight but I'm OK,' he says.

'Do you need any more pain killers or anything?'

He doesn't, but I ask because all I care about now is that he doesn't suffer too much pain. I want him to feel nothing and to be able to slip away quietly when the time comes.

Dad is becoming noticeably weaker, he's losing the fight for life and I keep thinking of how his final moments will be and pray that it is not agonising for him. I can't bear the thought of him having to endure a long, slow, drawn-out death. I don't want to see him suffer. That's the fear with cancer. It spells distress and agonising pain. I hate the word. I fear it. It's one of the reasons that although I am in my late-thirties I *still* don't smoke in front of my parents. It seems ludicrous to be that old and still have to sneak outside for a cigarette...but cigarettes mean cancer and I don't want them to worry about my health.

I'm also a terrible hypochondriac – any twinge, ache or pain and I have always been convinced that a painful death from cancer is just around the corner. I have been for several scans already and will have another one just a month after my Dad passes away.

For now, cancer has indeed come home to roost – but not in a seasoned smoker like me; instead it has chosen my father – a man whose lifestyle has been the polar opposite of mine – my father never smoked, rarely drank to excess, and ate a fresh and healthy three meals a day. I smoke like a trooper, binge-drink with abandon, and eat junk food to survive. If I was to be struck down with cancer, then fair enough. But Dad: he's done nothing to deserve this.

As he sleeps upstairs, I speak to my brother on the phone. Dad's illness has come at the worst time for Adam. He works on a farm and this time of year is one of the busiest for him. He's been totally bogged down and hasn't been able to get any time off. He is desperate to see Dad and was planning on coming home at the weekend but says he may be able to find time to come round for supper that evening. I urge him to do so because I know that Dad is deteriorating fast and I want Adam to see him while he is still able to talk without too much trouble.

When he arrives, Adam goes upstairs and sits down to speak to Dad. I can hear the faint echo of their voices as I walk around the kitchen helping Mum prepare supper. I hate the fact that Adam has to leave Dad and come back down to the kitchen alone. I want Hamesy to be able to eat with us but he can't. Instead, Dad is now hardly even moving in the confines of his bed, lying static on his right hand side in the place where Mum used to sleep.

We sit down to eat and I am so glad that my brother and I can still make each other laugh. But it seems odd, that although we are all cast in the shadow of grief and our hearts weigh heavy, we are still able to enjoy ourselves as our Dad lies dying upstairs. But I'm thrilled too, because I know Dad can hear us and I want him to hear some joy in his final days of life.

It's great having Adam home for that evening. Adam is our own private court jester, the comedy ace up the family sleeve and he charms us all with amusing anecdotes and stories about his life in Warwickshire. I take the mickey out of him and his grin spreads into laughter and I love the fact that Adam has been able to lift us all. Adam leaves later that night and we all feel much better for having seen him.

Time

In the months following the death of my father, I will cast my mind back to a time several years ago when he was waiting for me at Telford train station. I had some time off work and had returned home one day for some rest and re-hab. He is standing, smiling, and ready as always with a welcoming *'Hello lad.'*

When we get back to the house, Dad tells me about a speech he is due to give to the local geological society. As we're chatting, I notice he has a strange tickly cough – he has had this before over the last few years but it has got a little worse now and continually fractures his sentences with mini-hiccups. It sounds funny and makes me burst into laughter. It's like he has what appears to be the residue of a cold and sounds a little bit like a scratched record, and I can't resist from giving him some stick. I rib him a little and question whether he's in any fit state to give a speech when he can't even reach the end of a single sentence properly.

At the same time, I'm genuinely interested in what he'll be talking about - Dad's enthusiasm for geology, which he studied at university, has been rekindled by my parents' move to Much Wenlock, home to some historic geological sites.

I manage to persuade him to give me and Mum a dress rehearsal speech in the living room. I suspect this may turn into something of a comedy routine so I press 'record' on my camera video phone.

Dad begins his speech and is immediately beset with mini-hiccups. It's hilarious. I am trying to clamp my mouth shut so that I don't laugh out loud and ruin the recording. I see Mum sitting opposite my Dad and she's grinning ear-to-ear, her eyes sparkling. I can hold back no longer and neither can Mum; we burst out laughing. Even though Dad is close to hysteria himself, he is still trying to struggle through his script. He is shaking with laughter while talking and eventually he has to stop and, standing there, he is soon crying with laughter and it's a delightful sight.

It's such a bittersweet memory because months after Dad has died I will learn that the hiccupping dry cough which had made me laugh so much was almost certainly an early symptom of his fatal illness. And although I try not to let this taint such a happy memory, I know it's unavoidable. Oh! If only we had known.

Eventually, we manage to compose ourselves and he reaches the end of his hiccup-infested talk. I make a few suggestions for changes to the script but I have found it really illuminating.

The essence of his speech lies in helping to illustrate that what we consider to be permanent and solid parts of the landscape, are in fact transient objects. Buildings, walls, rocks, even mountains and whole continents – all will move and change, some will eventually be whittled away, morphed and completely eroded by time and nature. He begins by saying that rock-dating technology puts the earth at 4 billion years old. If that timeframe was to be considered a 24 hour clock then the time from now back to the year 3000 BC would amount to just a few minutes on the stopwatch.

I suggest to him that if that's the case, if he was to click his fingers at the start of the speech then that would be less than the equivalent of a single human lifetime.

And when I think about this later, now that he has died, I am beset with morbid, depressing thoughts about how little time we all have, that the years flash by and it's all over in an instant, just when we're finally getting to grips with everything. When we are young we think a lifetime is an age, that we'll never really reach the end of it; but of course, we all do. None of us, despite the fact that we continually kid ourselves otherwise, will be an exception to the rule of history – everyone will die. One day you and I really will be the body in that coffin; one day that memorial service will be for us; and one day, hundreds of years from now, even the stone on that grave of ours will eventually crumble and fall to earth.

These days though, we seem to spend half our time on a government-sponsored health drive in order to achieve longer life-spans, as if on an impossible drive to achieve everlasting life. We are discouraged from overeating and told not to drink too much. We are banned from smoking in public places, and we're told to eat 'five a day'. Health scares are becoming ever more common and ever more extreme. I even recently read a newspaper article where it said that drinking hot tea increases the risk of cancer of the oesophagus. I'm not joking – this is the transcript from Bloomberg News:

'Compared with drinking the beverage four or more minutes after being poured, drinking tea less than two minutes after pouring was associated with a fivefold higher risk of cancer, according to the study findings.'

The report goes on to advise us *'to wait four minutes before drinking your next hot beverage.'* Yeah, right, I'm there with my cup of tea, a thermometer and a stopwatch. It's ridiculous.

I'm not necessarily disputing these findings; I'm just saying I would prefer to live a little bit rather than to be constantly living in fear of my impending death. Maybe this is all a bit confusing: here I am banging on about death and dying and now I'm having a go at a medical profession which is giving me what could be valuable insights into how to stay alive longer. But the fact is, I feel as though I can handle the despair; it's the hope that's dangled in front of me that I can't cope with. It's like supporting the England football team – promises, promises....but we all know how the story ends.

What I really want is to be left alone to live in peace. I don't want to be constantly bombarded with new data to tell me the statistical risks of my lifestyle and behaviour. I don't want to be told how to avoid what I fear most. I'd rather bury my head in the sand and take what's coming to me and hope that I can meet it head on with grace and wit. When so-called experts are hauled out to illustrate the link between cancer and smoking it makes me reach for yet another cigarette mainly to help combat the stress of having just heard how high-risk I am. That's a pretty vicious circle.

But what's it matter anyway? - These health drives are just postponing what's inevitable: they're not a solution, just a delay strategy. And if I'm going to die, then I'd rather get on with living without constantly assessing my prospects of survival. What difference does it make if I die tomorrow, in ten years, or in one hundred years' time? Do I really want to live forever? - In some ways I do – of course I do - but not if it means that I have to become physically old and decrepit. I'm such a spoiled brat: I want all the rewards, all the time in the world, but I don't want any of the hassle or pain that comes with it.

Poor Dad, I wish he'd just lived a little longer. He was such a good guy, and funny too. One time when I go home to see my parents, I have a video camera with me to take footage of Dad to submit to a TV production company who are making a programme, *Kitchen Criminals*, about people who can't cook. Dad will manage to illustrate this perfectly by taking out a bottle opener to try and open a tin of tomatoes. It's priceless.

My camera will be going into steady-cam facility overdrive as I shake with laughter when Dad finally finishes his somewhat suspect dish of spaghetti bolognese and reaches down to pick up the plate - only to burn himself and then collapse in hysterics. And now, all that joy, fun, life and laughter is left only on a videotape, which in turn, like everything else, will eventually, in time, decay and dissolve into dust.

Fear of Flying

I wonder what Dad is thinking as he lies in bed. He's always been a deep thinker, a philosophical type. He was more spiritual and moral rather than religious; but he must be thinking about what lies in wait after death has taken him from us. What must it be like for him to know that the end is lingering just around the corner? In truth, he doesn't seem in the least bit anxious, but there is sadness in his eyes. When I see him I don't prompt him into any leading discussions because all I'm really worried about right now, as always, is that he's not in pain. He seems at peace but I can tell he's looking ahead and he's missing us already. He's also talking less and less because tiredness sets in very quickly. I think he wants it over and done with, to just get through this as quickly as possible and rid himself of this illness, of the hassle and process of dying.

My father's all-too-obvious mortality transports me back to the only time I ever felt my own life was in any real kind of danger. I am in Brazil, South America, working on a television programme together with a camera crew and several contributors from the UK. Exhausted, we arrive at the airport desperate to leave for the next city where a hotel and a badly needed bed lie in wait. We look at each other with forlorn resignation - outside is a small runway being pounded with huge dollops of tropical rainfall.

A tannoy announcement confirms our worst fears of yet another delay to our flight and yet more hanging around in limbo.

'Oh, bloody hell.'

'Agreed,' I hear from Kyle.

Flashes of lightning light up the static plane outside. Lashings of rain snake down in violent streams across the window. Maybe it's not such a good idea to fly after all. A couple of hours pass and there is still no let-up in the weather. I settle down to sleep on the floor but am quickly brushed to my feet by Kyle.

'Ash, we're off. They've just called the flight.'

One of the contributors rushes up to us.

'We can't fly in this weather! It's madness! Come on guys - look outside.'

She's right – great drops of water are falling like stones into vast patches of flooding. Flashes of lightning are visible in the distance.

'If this was England,' she adds, 'there's no chance they would be flying in this. No way am I getting on that flight!'

The thought of spending the entire night in an airport lounge fills me with even more dread than a risky flight. I want to get going and move to reassure her.

'They wouldn't call the flight if they weren't sure it was safe to fly. Come on, let's go.'

We head off to join the queue.

As we take our seats in the plane my enthusiasm for taking off begins to turn to dread. This is starting to feel very wrong. Kyle takes the seat in front of me and across from me sits Cat, our assistant producer. A crash of thunder sounds in the background and we look outside and then back at each other.

I try to lighten the mood.

'Just remember folks', I say tongue-in-cheek, 'it's the first and last couple of minutes of a flight that are the most dangerous. As long as we get through the take-off and landing we'll be right as that rain out there.'

I'm being facetious. One of the contributors throws me a look of daggers and starts to cry.

'Shut up Ashley!'

'Oh God, I'm sorry. I didn't mean it. Come on, we'll be fine. Seriously, they wouldn't fly unless it was safe.'

'I don't feel safe,' she replies, cutting me down to size.

'It'll be alright,' I say, as much to myself as to anyone else.

Whatever we think, it's too late to back out now. The engines have started - there's no turning back unless we create a scene. But hey, we're English - we're not going to do that. We're going to keep our feelings to ourselves; important things will be left unsaid. Same old story, really.

Engines to full, we're racing down the runway. Another brief flash of lightning illuminates the outside and I can see strips of rainfall thrashing onto the ground. Rain is literally bouncing off the windows. There is silence on board. Everyone bar none is feeling very uneasy about this. Soon, we are in mid-air and flying.

But this is to be no ordinary flight.

The sense of vulnerability is acute. The plane feels totally out of control, twisting and pitching violently as we gather height racing through black, heavy clouds. This is not normal. In fact, it's bloody terrifying. I feel like I am in a death trap – it feels no longer like a plane, just a fragile metal tube flailing through space.

I look across at Cat and she is sitting in silence, tears gently falling down her cheeks as her body shudders in her chair. It's obviously not just me who is filled with genuine alarm – we are all feeling helpless. Our seats are starting to clatter as the plane pitches and jolts. I put my hand on Kyle's shoulder and he turns a fraction and nods reassurance but says nothing. We're way up high now and still there is no equilibrium, no stability, we're shifting from side to side, up and down.

It feels like we're hurtling through space, not flying through air.

The plane shudders and I can see panic on people's faces, and it must be on mine too – I am very, very scared. The pilot must absolutely 100 per cent be regretting the decision to take-off and fly. But we're committed now – an aborted flight at this point would be suicidal. We push onwards and upwards, the wings twitching and battling to stay steady. This is not happening is it? It is.

It seems like we are going to crash.

I think one of the wings may snap off and we will spiral out of control.

Shrieks from frightened passengers fill the air. I can't bear the thought that if we start to free-fall to our deaths that people will be screaming – I just want to remain in silence and go quietly to my death.

I put my hand again on Kyle's shoulder and give him a squeeze. He turns his head slightly.

'You alright Ash?'

'Yeah. Sort of.'

The plane jolts violently. It's petrifying. I hear a muffled scream from the back of the plane. I imagine the pilot wrestling with the controls in the cockpit: so far, so good. Sort of. I look out of the window and wisps of dark, angry clouds race past. The light on the end of the wings flashes in the darkness and thick rain is pelting past. It seems like we are going ridiculously fast. I am expecting to see the oxygen masks fall down from above our seats at any second.

I have no thoughts, just a wish that I survive or die. Like my Dad, I just want to get through this alive and in one piece or get my death over and done with. I don't think about the meaning of life or God or anything – things are moving too fast for that – there's just a great big, simple nothingness going through my head.

Then, quite suddenly, we break through the clouds and things seem to settle down. The plane begins to level out and I know then that the worst is over. I feel like I've been holding my breath for twenty minutes and I can breathe easier now.

'Are you OK Cat?' I ask.

Cat looks back at me and nods. Kyle reaches over to her, holds her arm and another tear escapes and rolls down her face.

'It's only an hour's flight', Kyle reminds her. 'We'll be there soon.'

And we are there soon and we can rest easy. We've landed, we're alive and well and I feel like life is a crazy bloody thing but it's damn well worth living and I'm glad I'm still part of it.

We gather up our bags and as we walk out of the airport I feel a hand on my shoulder and the voice of Kyle behind me:

'I love you Ash.'

I love hearing these words. I turn around and Kyle steps next to me. I look at him as we walk.

'I love you too Kyle.'

And I still need to say these words to my Dad, is what I'm thinking right now.

141

DAY SIX

The Cross

I have already told Dad that I want to be there when he passes away, that I want to be with him when he is taken from his bed at home and goes to the hospice to die. The next day, when I speak to him about this, he seems surprised but I insist that I have thought it through and that I *need* to be there with him. I have told Mum too and she understands. I want to somehow pay Dad back in small part for everything that he has done for me, to help comfort him in his final moments. I also feel I should be there for Mum as well. Neither of us has seen anyone die before and that first person will be my father and her husband.

We feel like we're in this together and we will go with Dad right to the end.

Dad tells me he was offered the opportunity to see his own father after he had died but declined to visit the body for fear that his last memory of his father was of a dead person in a morgue. He wanted to remember his father alive. He is suggesting to me that perhaps it's not such a good idea that I witness his death.

'I want to be there with you Dad.'

Hamesy looks at me affectionately and says that if that's how I feel then he's fine with that. He adds that he's heard that the actual moment of death is supposed to be a peaceful moment. I agree, saying that I have heard that too, and I really hope against hope to myself that this truly will be the case for Dad.

Downstairs, I browse through some of the letters and cards which Mum has opened earlier in the day. One of them is from a Catholic priest and beside it on the table is a small, wooden cross. In the accompanying card is written the heartfelt suggestion to Dad that the more he feels his life slipping away, the more tightly he should grip the cross. The words are written with real love and compassion but it leaves me desperately fearful that Dad is going to suffer and be in pain during the process of dying. I have nightmare scenarios of seeing his skeletal figure festering in the hospice, of him being upset and struggling for breath, of clutching the cross and screaming in agony.

He is such a gentle, sweet and thoughtful man and I can't cope with thinking that this is the possible fate that awaits my father. He deserves so much better than that.

I speak to Mum about the cross. I think most days she is taking one or two letters or cards up to show Dad so I ask her if she will be taking this one up for him to see. She says that she won't be taking it up yet and I know that the time for her to deliver it will be the time when she senses that Dad is about to lose his battle for life.

Mum is being so good, so impressive, so dignified, and I find it impossible to fathom how devastated she must be feeling. When I ask her how she is, she answers by saying that she simply feels 'incredibly sad.' And that pretty much sums up how I think we're all feeling.

It feels like our senses have been thrust onto an assault course: we are feeling emotions from depths we never even knew existed. We are forgetful, agitated, but above all, consumed by sadness.

Our grief is sometimes manifesting itself in quite bizarre ways. I find myself sighing a huge amount and it's something that I can't shake. They are not just small sighs – they emanate from the gut. I notice Mum and Rebecca frequently sighing as well and begin to realise it's just a normal physical reaction to the intense pain we are all feeling. There are so many battling emotions trapped in the air we breathe out: frustration, pain, anticipation, fear, and deep and almost unbearable melancholy.

Conversely, there are passages of time in which I feel nothing, when I feel OK. I watch TV and read the newspapers or a book and am able to immerse myself in them without thinking about Dad. And then I catch myself being carefree, enjoying myself, and suddenly I am overcome with guilt. Why am I feeling alright when my father is upstairs dying? Does this mean I don't care enough? Am I heartless or is this normal?

I mention this to Mum and she says that she hasn't read anything or really watched any TV since Dad became ill. She is dislocated, unable to focus on things which now seem completely pointless and insignificant.

We are all very distracted and absent-minded. My mother will go to the fridge and by the time she gets there she will have no idea what it was she wanted. I sometimes read the same page of a book several times over before I suddenly realise I've read it just seconds before.

We are muddled, confused, overloaded with too much information, too much emotion.

Conversations are sometimes bizarre meanderings where we forget what we are talking about mid-sentence. Words travel through space and fail to register. I will have a chat to Mum about what she is cooking for supper and just a few seconds later I will ask her what we're having for supper. She will look at me quizzically and say that we have just been talking about that. I won't have any recollection of it whatsoever. Luckily, this is to such an extreme degree that we find humour in it because it is kind of comical. It's all so surreal and we feel like we're all going a bit bonkers, so we pull silly faces and giggle a bit and then shrug our shoulders as we think that this is what it's like when the world is falling to pieces in front of you.

Pop

I am at home in London, present time. I check my voicemail in the afternoon and there is a message from my Mum asking me to call her. There is no more information but I know instantly from her tone of voice that she is ringing me because my grandfather Pop has taken a turn for the worse. I knew this call was coming. I call her back and ask her the news. She has just returned home from visiting her father in hospital: it doesn't look good.

'I'm afraid your grandfather may well be breathing his last breaths tonight,' she tells me.

Her voice does not falter and it seems she has become acclimatised to this latest emotional battering. And I too feel ready to hear that Pop may well be nearing the end. We have expected this for some time now.

'OK Mum', I say.

'I think you kids knew this was going to happen so I just thought I'd warn you.'

'Sure,' I say, 'thanks for letting me know.'

Mum and I chat for a while. She explains that Pop has now been moved to a private room in the hospital. This, I assume, is so that the other patients in the hospital are protected from witnessing an actual death in front of their eyes. He is on heavy medication and is barely conscious, unable to communicate and without the strength to eat. The doctors have switched to giving him palliative care – to relieve his suffering rather than to hold out any hope that he will survive for much longer.

I ask Mum if she is alright and she admits to feeling exhausted and worn out but I think she is prepared for this – it's been a long time coming. The only surprise for us is that it's Pop who looks like he'll be the first to go rather than my grandmother Petal who has, for the last decade, always appeared the more fragile of the two.

I ask Mum about Petal and whether she has been made aware that her husband is seriously ill. Over the past few months Petal has herself deteriorated – physically she is still in one piece, albeit confined to a wheelchair – but mentally she is increasingly awry. She responds to questions but everything is quickly forgotten. Dementia has set in. She does not seem particularly disoriented, she is just....there.

She has become a vessel, something of a vacuum, a body without any real function.

During my more recent visits I can sometimes detect the spark of the spirit we once knew but these are rare moments: it seems she is just passing the time, waiting to move on and disappear. She is at the point where death means very little to her now, other than a release.

Mum tells me that even though her parents have spent well over seventy years together and – barring Pop's service in World War 2 - scarcely a day apart, Petal has not once asked where he has gone and why he is missing from the care home. This seems extraordinary: since they moved there a couple of years ago they have spent virtually every minute of every day together – how can Petal not have noticed his absence? It's clear however, that her dementia is now at an advanced stage. Despite this, I wonder out loud if she should be told that Pop is in a critical situation but Mum explains that she has been advised by the care nurses that Petal should not be told anything yet, unless she explicitly asks for information. They are worried that being so old, any upsetting news could threaten her well-being.

It feels odd for me as a grandchild to know more about Pop's whereabouts and the state of his health than his own wife but this is how things are. I finish my chat with Mum and tell her I will call her tomorrow to check how things have gone.

That evening I take my new girlfriend out for a drink and meet with some friends for a catch-up. It seems bizarre that I am still be able go out and enjoy myself. While I stand at the bar laughing and drinking, I know that simultaneously my grandfather is in a desperately ill condition in a hospital hundreds of miles away in Shropshire. I wonder if I should feel guilty about this but I know that Mum was aware I had plans that evening and wanted me to go out and have fun and not concern myself too much with her or with Pop.

When I go outside on my own for a cigarette her words echo in my thoughts again:

'Your grandfather may well be breathing his last breaths tonight.'

For me, life goes on; but for my grandfather it is about to end.

The next day I wake up late and there is another message from Mum. I have to call her back and I already know exactly how this conversation will pan out:

'Mum. It's me.'

Mum comes straight out with it.

'I'm afraid he died yesterday evening.'

'Oh Mum, I'm so sorry.'

'Well, I'm sorry I didn't tell you last night but I knew you were going out and...'

'That's fine, don't worry about it. What happened?'

Mum explains that Pop had died just a couple of hours after she had spoken to me. She had a call from the hospital a few hours after visiting him for the last time and it was all over.

'We're both without Dads now,' Mum says to me.

The words strike home and I feel a hammer blow of searing isolation. I can't come close to even comprehending just how awful Mum must feel now that both her husband and father have gone in such a short space of time. All I wish is that Dad was now alive to look after her. But he's not and there's nothing I can do about that. Mum and I talk for a while and quickly discuss plans for me to come home. I can feel myself starting to feel upset and I don't want Mum to hear me cracking up so I move the conversation forwards and say my goodbye.

I put the phone down and I look up towards the ceiling of my living room and for just a couple of seconds I feel an incredible sense of disappointment that a life, the life of my grandfather, has just gone. In those seconds I am reminded of my father and how I felt when he died - the feeling of emptiness, of isolation, of fear that this person, my father and now my grandfather, has now gone to nothing. What seemed like substantive, meaningful lives have just disappeared into thin air, dissipated into space, and all that's left are memories, photographs and old clothes.

I look ahead of me and two tears roll down my cheeks. But this time, a close bereavement in the family, although it injects me with a brief shot of angst and sense of futility, is somehow different. Before long, I am back to feeling more relaxed, relieved even: I feel far, far better attuned to the death of my grandfather. Unlike in my Dad's case, this feels like it was for the good – Pop was, as Mum had said earlier on the phone, 'not a happy man.'

And this is true: I think Pop would gladly have dispensed with the last couple of years of his life and taken an early exit if he had had the chance. His death has meant the end of his suffering, an end to the tears, the confusion and the pain. It has also been a relatively quick process after a short stay in hospital and Mum is not left having to make endless trips to visit him and fret over his condition. Relief, not grief is my overriding emotion.

But I wonder how will Petal feel? How will she react? She has already been told that Pop is in hospital but the nurses aren't sure if the information has fully registered with her. When and how will they go about telling her that Pop's life is now over? A couple of days later we get the answer. One of the care nurses is chosen to break the news to Petal. It is morning and Petal has been woken up to have her breakfast. She is helped into a wheelchair and then the nurse leans over her and quietly says that she has some bad news - that Pop has been very ill but has lost his battle and has died.

Petal listens and then is quiet. A single tear rolls down her face. The nurse asks her if she is alright.

Petal answers her, 'Yes, thank-you.'

'Would you like some breakfast?'

'Yes please.'

Petal is taken through to the dining area where she is given her breakfast.

The death of her husband is never mentioned again.

Thank You

Dad needs an increasing amount of morphine to stave off the pain of the cancer. This means he is sleeping a lot more, but when he is awake he seems in good spirits. He seems so peaceful and is still able to smile when we go in to see him. He is still talking as well, and in the morning when I walk past the bedroom I see Rebecca there with him. Dad is dictating a letter which he wants her to send off to all his business associates. When I later go up to Dad's office to check my emails, I see a copy of the letter sitting on the desk. It begins with him telling his customers:

'I'm afraid time is not on my side: I have been given a matter of weeks rather than months left to live...'

It again reinforces that this is so real, that there is no getting out of this, no magic wand that we can wave. I sigh, pause, and think to myself how hard these words must have been for Rebecca to hear and to write down. My sister is being an absolute star and I can see that Dad's practical approach to life has rubbed off on his daughter. Like Mum, she too is a fighter.

I head back inside to see Dad and again he checks to see if I have managed to send off some stock from the office. His obsession with his small business affairs is, somewhat comically, reaching biblical proportions – Mum and I later raise our eyebrows when he mentions it for the umpteenth time that day. But in a way, I think it's also a really healthy distraction – it's giving us all something to focus on which we can actually deal with, rather than with the problem of terminal cancer which none of us can solve.

Occasionally though, when I see him, I will prompt Dad to talk to me about something other than spread-sheets and cardboard boxes. I keep trying to help him see the positive side of his situation - he has so much to be thankful for, he's been really healthy and happy and if I could have had his life I would have happily swopped him for it. But in truth, as I tell him this, it's not really Dad that I'm reassuring – he quite plainly doesn't need any reassurance – the person I'm trying to pep up, to help come to terms with his illness, is actually myself.

Dad asks me how I am feeling and if I am OK and as I begin to respond I can't stop myself from crying. When I have recovered myself he will ask me if all the stock from the office has been sorted out, and I can't stop myself from smiling.

As I stand there near him, all I really want is to lie down next to him and hold his hand and hug him and settle down with him. Again, I want to tell him I love him and I want him to say the same back, but a mixture of shyness and wanting to just let him be stops me. As time has moved on and his condition has worsened I am increasingly aware of trying not to add to his discomfort by burdening him with any awkward moments, with anything he may find difficult to say. Or is this just my excuse for being too emotionally repressed?

I'm still frustrated and annoyed at myself for not biting the bullet to actually tell my dying father, 'Dad, I love you.' And time is running out.

But I at least I am able to sit there and be with him for a while, so we talk a little and I gather myself up to say thank you to him. This is one of the things that I have written on my list of 'Things to Say to Dad.' I have written this down because I know Dad sacrificed a lot for us. He had always been totally committed to his family, and although his role was always appreciated, I, for one, had not always thanked him for it.

'I just want to say, from me and also, if they don't get a chance to say it, from Adam and Rebecca, that we thank you for everything Dad,' I say.

He thanks me for saying that and says that 'thank you' can sometimes be a difficult thing to express.

Not as difficult as 'I love you.'

I still haven't said this and I still have my little list of things to say to my Dad. Everything has now been crossed off except that.

I look over at him – in the dim light his eyes are fierce, burning bright, terminal cancer eyes. I can't believe that it has come to this, that this is how my father will die. He seems too young in years but in the last week he has started to look physically much older – just like I had told my sister, he is beginning to resemble his own father, his grey thinning hair is looking softer, wispy. His skin is pale, yellowish. I don't like to see the colour of yellow in the whites of his eyes; it's a vivid reminder of just how ill he is.

But his eyes are still so keen to stay open, to look at me and to connect.

He has light grey stubble which I have never seen on him before. I notice too that he is now much thinner. I see that the flesh on his arms is starting to hang looser; his face is beginning to look slightly hollow and the bridge of his nose is more pronounced from weight loss. He is eating miniscule amounts of food – anything substantial is swiftly thrown up. He is also rejecting the food supplements that Mum is trying to give him because he doesn't like the taste.

The supplements are important though – this is what will give my father the energy to continue his fight for life, and we are trying desperately to keep him alive for longer. There's huge conflict here – we don't want to extend his agony any more than necessary but we also can't bear the thought of him dying.

For the time being, Mum is satisfied that he is not suffering too much - the morphine is doing its job. This being the case, when Dad asks for something to drink, Mum immediately kicks into action downstairs, mixing powdered protein into his drinks to give him extra nutrients. This becomes a rich seam of humour as she plots away in the kitchen to fix him up a drink, trying to inject the maximum amount of additives without Dad noticing the disparity in taste. I am the designated taste detective. Mum piles in the powder and then gives it a good stir. But she's put so much in it that the protein won't fully dissolve and I can see it clearly visible, clotted around the surface of the drink. If Dad sees this, he will immediately reject it because he doesn't like how it tastes. We pour that one down the sink and try another, but Mum has put too much in again, the drink tastes awful and we'll have to throw that one away as well.

'Come on Mum! Hurry up!'

A third time and she gets the right mix; I taste it, give it the go-ahead and she delivers it upstairs. Dad will look at her, take a sip and ask if she has once again been messing around with his drinks order – why has it taken us over ten minutes to bring him up an orange juice?! Mum denies it; but Dad knows and drinks it anyway.

Mum will come downstairs and, as our eyes meet there is a sense of triumph and we do a mental high five: we have just won ourselves some more time.

Despite our best efforts, however, Dad is now looking increasingly fragile and pained, but he is still ready with a smile whenever we go in to see him. He has been at home for less than a week but he is already taking bigger doses of morphine and sleeping a lot more. I can sense that the end is drawing closer, perhaps faster than any of us realised.

I feel sorry that he is sleeping alone but I spoke to Mum about that yesterday and she has been in to see him during the nights to hold him, cuddle him and talk to him.

She has squared the circle and I think she is more or less ready.

Mum and I have spoken with Dad about plans for his funeral and memorial service. My father says he only wants a quiet family funeral – the money we would have spent on a fancy memorial service he wants donated to a charity to support a local boy with meningitis. When he says this he breaks down in tears but recovers himself quickly.

Mum mentions to him that I have said I would like to give the eulogy if we hold a memorial service, and he asks me if this is the case. 'Yes Dad,' I say.

Then I try to find the words to explain that I want to give him the send-off I feel he deserves but all I manage to say is that *'I just want to say: "Brilliant"'*.

And as I say this, I motion with my hands as if I am actually giving that speech and I am pointing towards an imaginary coffin placed at the altar of the church. But I am sitting in my Dad's bedroom and I am looking out of the window towards the garden.

Dad looks proudly towards me and I can tell he's surprised but happy to hear that I have resolved to speak on his behalf. We reach the conclusion that we will have the small family funeral as he wishes but he has given his seal of approval if we also decide to hold a memorial service as well.

The phone rings downstairs and Mum leaves us. I stay on with Dad and ask him if there is anything that needs to be said between us. In my head, I'm urging him to tell me he loves me so I can say it back to him and feel that everything is complete. He looks up at me and says that of his three children it is with me that he has had 'the most difficult relationship' so he tells me he's happy I was here to work a few things out with him.

I know what he means.

As I write this I'm tempted to change the word 'difficult' that Dad uses and replace it with 'least easy,' because although me and Dad had the occasional difference, we always got on pretty damn well. We had always been quite competitive, independent and free-spirited so we could sometimes step on each other's toes. Our similarities meant there was often some rivalry but deep down we were very close. And over the last few years, I think we had found a more even keel.

Dad, at 67, was mellowing with age and was just on the verge of developing into a lovely old man, while at thirty years younger I was starting to appreciate him that little bit more.

Like Dad just said, I'm glad too because being with him at this time has meant that we have had the opportunity to spend some valuable time with each other, to understand each other just that little bit more, to tighten our bond together. We have done this and I am happy it is done and Dad reassures me of that. He says we have no unfinished business and I well up with happiness as he says that.

I still want to tell him that I love him but, again, I don't. I feel better though and more relaxed, so I go back upstairs, put myself to bed, and sleep soundly for the first time in weeks.

DAY SEVEN

The End

It's Friday, and Adam is coming back home tomorrow for the weekend. We're all looking forward to being a complete family again for the short amount of time that Dad has left.

Dad is being sick a lot and Mum is in the bedroom looking after him.

During the day, I walk up and down the stairs a few times, ostensibly to go to my bedroom to make some phone calls, but in truth, it's so I can walk past my parents' room to keep an eye on things. One time as I walk slowly past, I see Mum at his bedside and she looks more worried than I have ever seen her before. I stop at the door and mouth 'OK?' and Mum nods back.

I don't want to intrude, so I leave them alone.

In the afternoon, I pass by again and Mum is still in there looking after him. I head up to my bedroom to try and have a quick snooze but as I near the door I slow down and eventually stop. Standing there above my father I say quietly, *'I love you Dad,'* because I still haven't said this to him and I want to hear myself say it out loud. I want to be able to look back and think, *'Yes, I said it, even though Dad could not hear me.'*

For the moment, and perhaps for ever, this will have to do.

I wake up later and find that Dad is still suffering badly - he's vomiting a lot and Mum is trying to sooth him and help him rest. When I go and check up on him later, I see that Dad has finally fallen asleep, so I leave him and go back down to the kitchen for supper. I think about whether I should perhaps phone Adam and alert to him the fact that Dad has taken a turn for the worse, but he's due to arrive tomorrow morning anyway and I don't want to alarm him unnecessarily.

After eating, Rebecca and I go next door where I watch some TV and my sister settles down to read. At one point, Mum comes down and I can tell she's extremely worried – Dad is very unsettled and is unable to hold down any morphine. She decides to phone Shrop-Doc, a local twenty-four-hour medical emergency call-out service. After about ten minutes a Doctor arrives and I answer the door and take him upstairs. Mum is sitting at Dad's bedside and my father is looking desperately ill; he is very pale, with a cold flannel on his forehead to combat hot flushes and fever. There's a bowl ready by his chest in case he is sick. I ask the doctor if he is fully aware of my father's illness.

'Yes', he says, standing at the foot of the bed. 'Liver cancer: terminal.'

Those are the worst words to hear.

I leave him with my parents and return downstairs. I can't do anything to help and I don't want to interfere. I feel useless.

In just a single day, Dad's condition has gone downhill fast and it leaves me feeling very tense and nervous. The air somehow feels too light to breathe. Rebecca and I talk quietly for a while and then I see the Doctor out. Dad's body is rejecting anything that he takes orally so the Doctor has just injected Dad with some morphine in the hope that it settles into his bloodstream and allows him to rest.

After a short time, Mum comes down to see us and tells us the medication appears to have worked – Dad has finally crashed out. I feel a huge sense of relief because it means that he is no longer in any pain. I hope that tomorrow he will feel better and can enjoy some more time with Adam.

About half an hour later, Mum returns upstairs to check up on Hamesy while Rebecca and I sit on the sofa downstairs.

All of a sudden, we hear her cry out loud:
'Kids!'

Everything in our mother's voice is screaming out that Dad is perilously close to the end of the line. We spring out of our seats and run upstairs. I rush into the bedroom just ahead of Rebecca and we are greeted by the sight of Dad lying on his back, his head propped up on some pillows, looking straight ahead. Mum is lying next to him, her hand stroking his face.

Dad is moaning as he struggles to breathe. His breath is extremely laboured and comes in short, hard bursts in and out.

We rush in and as we crouch down on the side of the bed Rebecca says '*I love you, Dad.*'

In that moment I know in a flash that my sister has been thinking exactly the same as me.

Just as she finishes, I too say '*I love you, Dad.*'

We absolutely know that these are Dad's final moments.

Dad cannot speak. He is battling to breathe. Mum is talking gently to him, imploring him to let go, to stop fighting and not to worry about us, that we'll manage without him. She whispers to him that he has been an amazing, special person and a fantastic husband. Rebecca tells him what a brilliant father he has been and says that we are all here for him and that Adam is with us in spirit, his whole family here at his bedside.

Dad appears to be hanging on but he can't communicate. He's groaning, still breathing. Mum quickly suggests I try Shrop-Doc again. We're clutching at straws, desperate to help. I grab the phone and dial the number but for some reason the line is not working and I know that it's useless anyway, that Dad isn't going to make it. I shake my head at Mum and she understands.

I sit back down looking straight ahead at my father who is staring through me, breathing very hard now. I hold Dad's hand and tell him that it's OK for him to go, that we will miss him but that we will all be fine. My hand drops onto Dad's stomach and he moans louder this time and I am worried the weight of my hand on him is somehow hurting him so I lift my hand away. I look over at Mum who is nestling up against Dad telling him we all love him and saying there is no point in him trying to hang on, encouraging him to relax and to stop fighting for life.

Mum has said what we're all thinking, and my sister and I have finally told Dad that we love him. There will be no regrets.

Dad is really struggling to breathe. Bits of spittle fly from his mouth.

And then he stops breathing for several seconds and we stay silent.

These are agonising moments; tears are falling from my eyes and I can feel Rebecca's hand on my shoulder. Then a huge breath is taken in and exhaled. Dad's jaw has gone limp, his lips tremble as air is sucked in. But then, another long, endless pause, and he takes one more breath. I think that perhaps Dad has already died, that his spirit has gone but his body is taking slightly longer to do so, that this is just reflex.

Lungs that have been breathing for 67 years are still trying to do their job, to take in oxygen.

Then, after what seems like an age, but is probably five seconds or so, another breath is taken in and breathed out.

Then, there is silence; nothing.

We don't move and then I hear Rebecca asking me to close Dad's eyes. I wait for a few more seconds because although I'm pretty sure that my father has died, I want to be one hundred per cent certain. I put my hand on his chest and hold it there, trying to feel for a heartbeat.

There is nothing.

Everything is still.

I look over at Mum, who is holding her husband in her arms.

'He's dead,' I say.

We stay still together for a moment and then I reach over to close my father's eyes. I can see that one of his pupils is slightly off-centre as though an electric shock - a bolt of lightning - has coursed through his body, like a robot that has malfunctioned.

Rebecca moves over to my mother; they hug and Mum tells her daughter she loves her, and then as I walk over to her to kiss her she tells me she loves me too, and for the first time in my life, I say 'I love you too Mum.'

We sit together for a minute or two and we can't quite believe what has happened: that Dad has just died in front of our eyes, right here in my parents' bedroom.

In just a single week, we have hurtled from an initial diagnosis to my father dying from cancer.

The body which lies there now seems oddly irrelevant - we have the almost tangible sensation that Dad is absent, gone forever, and although he is still on the bed, it's not really him – it's a body, nothing else. Its presence however, is a silent witness to a family which will never be the same again.

We say a final goodbye, and as we leave the room, I sense that all my thoughts and fears that were previously occupied with my father have now perceptively shifted over to my Mum.

We gather downstairs in the lounge. It is now dark outside. I feel exhausted, but in the face of death, rather than feeling morbid, I am very much alert and alive. I feel like I have had an adrenaline rush. I think we are all in a massive state of shock. Mum declares that we could all use a glass of wine and that's the best idea I've heard all week, so we settle down for a drink.

I catch myself feeling oddly euphoric because I can't help but feel happy that Dad has reached the end without having to suffer for too long. As I look back, my thoughts are shot through with immense guilt - how can I possibly have felt anything other than sadness when my father has just died? Sitting there in the moments after he has died, I feel oddly energised, uplifted even – glad that our ordeal is over - but also very confused.

Mostly of course, I feel terribly sad - the death of my father seems so unfair, so premature; it seems such a waste of a good, productive life. Yet I also want to try to see this early death as his blessing – it was all over quickly and he died at home in bed surrounded by the people who loved him. And knowing that he heard us telling him we loved him also gives me tremendous solace. I'm grateful for the opportunity and feel like something truly significant both for me and for my Dad, was laid to rest right there in that moment of truth on my father's deathbed.

I'm grateful too that my father will now never have to suffer the afflictions of old age - he will never go deaf or blind, or battle with severe arthritis or dementia. He will never have to grieve the loss of his wife or any of his children; he will never have to grow old alone. Dad has seen the best of it, suffered a short illness, and then he left us, his struggle over. If death can in any sense be good, then this was a good death. This is my father's reward for a good life.

I can't help thinking that he was the lucky one - just as when he was in hospital, a mere seven days ago, it appears that all the problems, the consequences, the strife and the sorrow that descend when a loved one is lost – these are all fixed squarely on us, not him.

I think of how Dad's absence will cast a huge shadow over the joys I hope to see in the future – of perhaps falling in love, getting married, and having children. I will never again see the adorable grin on his face as I bring back an attractive girlfriend to seek his approval; he can no longer offer me advice on my career and help me carve out a secure and fulfilling future. He can no longer be there to witness my marriage, to hold my new-born baby, to be proud of any possible future achievements or successes that I, or my brother or my sister might have. And I worry that I will miss all that and that it will leave me castaway, without a rudder.

As I write these words, nearly two years after the anguish of witnessing my father reach the end of his life, I see death slightly differently. It still scares me. I loathe the thought that everything has to come to an end. But now, I look back at my Dad and succeed in finding some redemptive beauty in death, about the fact that we all have a limit to our existence. I am thankful that life is temporary – because that's exactly what helps to give life its meaning and to make it worth living. Death is what gives life an edge – it's the key to progress, it's what drives us forward, forces us to take action, to achieve, to leave our mark on the world. It's not life that impels us to get up in the morning, it's death.

And so, I no longer see the wrinkles around my eyes as a curse – I see them as battle scars.

I can also look back at how Dad continued to find joy after the death of his own parents and I feel more able to continue to lead a happy life, to crave new experiences and to relish the future. I find consolation for my Mum that my father's mother - my grandma - lived a full ten years after the death of her husband and that we would visit her and there would be laughter and happiness.

Of course, things will never be how they were when we were a complete family – and they were good times. Things will never be the same; they will be different for us all. And there is no getting away from the fact that we will feel real moments of despair. There will be times in the future when life will sometimes feel pointless, when nothing seems to really matter anymore. For the moment, and right up until the present time, it's true - we feel decimated. Our family is still functioning, but it's been disabled. It feels like a car with a wheel missing – it's moving forward but part of it will forever be scraping along the ground.

I still feel guilty that I had never told Dad that I loved him when he might have had the chance to respond. But at least it was said. I feel guilty of the cliché that before all this happened I took everything for granted. I remember Dad saying to me when I came home to visit that if ever he or Mum were to die suddenly and be taken from us then I should take a look in the top drawer of his desk. There, he said, I would find all the details of their will. At the time of course, I brushed it off with an 'OK Dad.' I thought it would never happen. But now I realise that these things really do happen. This is life, and nothing, absolutely nothing, is guaranteed.

As we sit on the sofa and the body of my father lies upstairs, I know as I look over at Mum that there is a long road ahead, full of unknowns and fraught with difficulties. But I think of how she has handled the past week and I am confident that she will cope, that eventually things will get better and that my mother will be able to come to terms with her loss.

And when I look at Rebecca, I feel the same. Later, in the months after Dad has died, Rebecca will be my support and give me the help I need and which I hope I showed her in the days leading up to Dad's death. She will end up showing me what an immensely strong, kind and lovely person she is. If nothing else, I am thankful for Dad's death for that clarity, for me being able to see that now because I didn't fully see it before.

We sit and we speak about my brother Adam who is due to arrive tomorrow, expecting to see his father alive, to talk to him and hold him. Now he won't get that chance and Mum is worried about how that may affect him. We wonder whether we should phone him but Mum decides that it's best not to: she doesn't want him driving back home in a state of distress; so instead I will break the news to Adam when he arrives in the morning. I will walk outside as I hear his car and as my brother approaches the front door I will say the words that will turn his face downwards and show such disappointment as I have never seen before:

'Dad died last night.'

As Mum, Rebecca and I share a glass of wine, there's a knock on the door and it's the doctor, returned to write out a death certificate for Dad. I deal with him and he does what he has to do and after showing him out, I pause before going back to Mum and Rebecca because I want to go back upstairs - I want to see Dad one more time before he is taken away by the undertakers. I can hear Mum and Rebecca talking quietly as I walk up the stairs and then I go into my parents' room where my father's body lies still in the bed.

I walk over to him and look down at his face. There is a single tear that has dropped from his right eye. It's such a sad sight for me to see. I hope it was not a tear from unhappiness at being torn apart from us, or from the physical pain of life being wrenched away from his body. I hope it is a tear of relief, a tear of joy and of hope. I gently wipe it away, and then I say goodbye for one last time and kiss his forehead.

'Goodbye Dad.'

His body is already starting to feel slightly cold; but in a few days' time for his funeral, it will be a warm, bright and beautiful sunny day.

MANY thanks for reading this.
If you enjoyed it, then please tell your friends.

You can connect with me here
www.twitter.com/ashleyhames
www.facebook.com/ashley.hames.3

To contact the author directly, please email
radarashley@yahoo.com

Copyright © 2011 Ashley Hames

All rights reserved.

Printed in Great Britain
by Amazon.co.uk, Ltd.,
Marston Gate.